INSPIRED
THINKING

INSPIRED THINKING

*Big Ideas to Enrich Yourself
and Your Community*

DOROTHY STOLTZ

WITH

Morgan Miller, Lisa Picker,
Joseph Thompson, and Carrie Willson

CHICAGO   2020

© 2020 by Dorothy Stoltz, Morgan Miller, Lisa Picker, Joseph Thompson, and Carrie Willson

Extensive effort has gone into ensuring the reliability of the information in this book; however, the publisher makes no warranty, express or implied, with respect to the material contained herein.

ISBN: 978-0-8389-4671-8 (paper)

Library of Congress Control Number: 2019040774

Cover design by Alejandra Diaz. Cover image © Adobe Stock.

Text design in the Chaparral, Gotham, and Bell Gothic typefaces.

⊗ This paper meets the requirements of ANSI/NISO Z39.48-1992 (Permanence of Paper).

Printed in the United States of America

24 23 22 21 20   5 4 3 2 1

To my baby grandniece, Adeline,
and to Helen Hubbard, lifelong learner
~ Dorothy

To the so-far-above-average
staff of Calvert Library
~ Carrie

Contents

PART III
IMPLEMENTING IDEAS

PART IV
FINDING THE LIGHT WITHIN IDEAS

Acknowledgments

Dorothy would like to thank her enlightened colleagues at the Carroll County (MD) Public Library, Maryland State Library and all Maryland libraries, Maryland Makes Collaborative, Maryland Family Engagement Coalition, and the Maryland STEM Festival. Special thanks to the American Library Association for building bridges among librarians, and to its many excellent divisions, including the Library Leadership & Management Association, the Public Library Association, and the ever cheerful Association for Library Service to Children. Thanks to everyone who helped the book team think things through, including Libraries Work and the superb staffers at Adele Coryell Hall Learning Commons at the University of Nebraska–Lincoln, Akron (OH) Public Library, the Mercantile Library of Cincinnati, Madison (WI) Public Library, University of Maryland, University of Washington, Kent State University, Allegheny County (Pittsburgh) Law Library, Richland (SC) Library, Boston Public Library, Maryland State Law Library, Northampton (PA) Middle School Library, Anne Arundel (MD) Public Law Library, and many more. Appreciation goes to inspirational treasures, such as the Library of Congress, New America, the Folger Shakespeare Library, Emerson House, and the Smithsonian. With special thanks to ALA Editions, especially Jamie Santoro, for their ongoing work to open doorways of wisdom for librarians.

Introduction

What is the role of libraries in an age of instant gratification? How can libraries design opportunities and environments to encourage people and enhance their ability to think, problem-solve, and learn? Since the early 1980s, rapid advances in technology have given people easy access to information and the ability to learn and work from anywhere. This has not trivialized the library, however; the world still needs libraries. Technology alone cannot guarantee the exploration of ideas that can lead to profound discoveries. Technology alone cannot help anyone to learn to think intelligently, critically, and holistically. Libraries continue to help humanity get to the big ideas.

It was our own response to the big ideas themselves that helped us conceive the idea for this book, which is centered on ideas that have stood the test of time—for example, curiosity, charity, and goodwill—and that have been implemented by great thinkers ranging from the ancient Greek philosophers to Alexander Pope, Ralph Waldo Emerson, and Abraham Lincoln. In this book, we are unabashedly promoting big ideas as a foundation for core values, perspectives, and a helpful mindset. But we are not promoting what people should think. We hope readers will learn to think for themselves.

Plato encourages us to go beyond forming an opinion in order to think through and activate big ideas such as contentment, gracefulness, and creativity. This book is a guide for leaders in any position and courageous followers in all types of libraries to tap the inspiration of big ideas and concepts.

The book starts with a prologue because this helps us set the tone for the rest of the text. Our prologue acts as a loving tip of the hat to Shakespeare. It was inspired by examples of the prologues used in Shakespearean plays. Prologues in Shakespeare feature a character or a chorus that comes out in front of the audience and gives an opening salvo. Our prologue serves the same purpose as the Shakespearean prologue—to set the stage and tone. We're celebrating and cheering with delight the wonders of libraries in order to prepare the reader to read and enjoy this book.

Part I of this book describes the importance of cultivating ideas, including Plato's definition of an idea—big and small—and the role of thinking. By developing inspired thinking and an open mind, libraries of all types can advance human achievement and the civilizing force of culture.

Part II guides us to find big ideas and build a bridge to them. By creating positive expectations and focusing attention on the powerful potential of libraries, we can create a healthy culture to activate the best in our staff and customers.

Part III shows how librarians are sitting on a treasure trove of big ideas, wisdom, awareness, and insights in their stacks, physical and virtual, and in their offerings of activities. Through these at-the-ready resources, librarians are poised to implement big ideas, such as courage and helpfulness, and help others learn about big ideas, and explore and express them.

Part IV is a call to action for library staffers to tap curiosity as a joyous quest for expanding our awareness and becoming more effective in life—when we grow first, then we inspire others. When individuals seek out resources at the library to read, ponder, and connect to the essence of big ideas—such as humility, joy, and unity—libraries can become the great treasure they are meant to be.

Pondering Plato and other great thinkers, Dorothy Stoltz, a community engagement director, studies the art of thinking with big ideas and how to apply them to libraries, organizations, and businesses. Library director Morgan Miller draws out the creative thinker in others and uses history as a touchpoint for inspiration to support people in the dream stage of an idea to help it become a reality. A master of event planning, Lisa Picker, communications director for a public library, implements ideas through teamwork and weaves a collaborative spirit into the fabric of the community. Influenced by Thomas Jefferson and Alexander Hamilton, Joe Thompson, a public services director, expects good things to happen, treasures an open mind for learning, and embraces value-added thinking. Library executive director Carrie Willson knows how to plan for the long term, advises other small and rural libraries, and enjoys reading great literature.

The concepts in this book are designed to generate interactions between big ideas and the needs of libraries and their customers—and to help us celebrate the enlightening of humanity.

Prologue

Whether it sits in a school, stands on the main street of a town, connects college lecture halls, or perches on the top floor of a hospital, the library—as a guidepost for light and wisdom—issues a call to action. It compels all—young and old—to expand what we know and can do. It persistently beckons us to explore life.

The library brightens the shadows with insight, wisdom, and joy for thinking things through. It embodies the "golden rule" of customer service: to treat others as we would like to be treated ourselves. The library discovers how to cherish those it serves so that its patrons—its clientele—its students—revere its purpose.

The library is not the possession of any one faction or group. It does not discriminate. It does not disrespect. Instead, the library promotes opportunity for all.

A true test of the library's commitment to the idea to "welcome all" occurs whenever the community is called to be tolerant and forgiving to those who are hostile and self-centered. At other times the library's dedication to "welcome all" is tested when we must cope with people from political, economic, and other groups who differ in some way from ourselves. These may be strangers to the library or to each other, but they may need assistance, encouragement, and inspiration. They need to discover that they can respect each other and get along. The library challenges itself and each of us to "welcome all," embracing the human impulse to grow and *celebrating life*.

A delight in improving our skills can soften the rough edge of doubt. Many of us discover the right book at the right time to solve a problem. However, the benefits of a library may not impact us overnight, but rather soak in gradually as we broaden our horizons. If we settle for instant gratification, we deprive ourselves of the transformative power of the library to enlighten humanity for the long haul.

A library does not judge. It surveys its community and comprehends the scene of diversity and at the same time the panorama of oneness. It poses opportunities to think, create, and bring out our best talents. Yet, it does not pester; instead, it nudges, nurtures, and nourishes by encouraging us to explore the many resources it offers.

The people's university—any library—kindles enthusiasm for learning. Through its informational treasures—classics and modern tomes, journal serials and newspaper archives, high-tech and low-tech resources—a library gives its customers the opportunity to learn and to grow. When correctly used through bibliographic instruction, experiential learning, and other engaging activities, the library expands curiosity, never shrinking it.

A lawyer may not know how to sift through the dross to discover research nuggets, but a librarian can help a law firm find the gold to produce excellent work. Without a library, we reduce a college's ability to inspire creativity; we sap a city's vitality; and we impair a school's capacity to teach children to become independent thinkers.

Humility, optimism, and cooperation are universal ideas to tap and express. Helpfulness, tolerance, and respect are designs of thinking that can generate opportunities for growth. The library is a beacon of light shining forth to make the seemingly impossible possible. Without a library, a town would become a dark place indeed. Folks from all walks of life may overlook whether a website is current, accurate, and authentic. But once they discover the library—and those of us working there—they are bound to notice the goodwill, expertise, and enthusiasm for asking the right questions that produce understanding and know-how.

With a hey, and a ho, and a hey nonino, we learners explore, discover, and grow. An iris grows each spring, blossoms, and eventually dies, but the inner essence of the iris continues on. The bulb maintains the nature of an iris and springs back to become a beautiful flower every year. Plato describes how opinions reflect our likes and dislikes but do not capture the inner essence of universal thinking or big ideas such as harmony, truth, and reverence.

A library increases our ability to understand big ideas. It brings forth streams of insight and restores our dreams. When up against opposition for financial support, the library turns inward to assess its service tone, its ability to listen and respond to customers, and its flexibility to collaborate.

The library is not self-absorbed or shortsighted; it works with big ideas, integrating them as much as possible into service to its community. It promotes unity, excellence, and the ability to know. It is greater than its physical facility, personnel, and educational resources. It works hand in hand with Shakespeare, Albert Schweitzer, and the like to clear away confusion and heal the distresses of the mind and heart.

The practice of medicine's big idea is maintaining health as opposed to focusing on healing sickness. A medical library helps its clientele stay attuned to its big picture. The practice of humility is to accept life, see the goodness in each situation, and use it as a springboard for growth and optimism. The library works with Mark Twain, Abraham Lincoln, and other practitioners of humility to help us increase our understanding and our ability to apply this ideal concept.

The library is a magnet drawing us into a realm that can elevate our capacity for learning, discovering excellence, and contributing to life. It encourages reflection. Collaborative workspaces and places to ponder can be found in today's top-notch library. No matter what our background or circumstances are, all of our boats can rise when we ask: What good can I do today? What good have I done this day? Ponder on this: every library, no matter whether it is academic, public, school, or specialty, helps us all to become wiser, more learned, more just, more everything.

The field of dignity is a realm open to all who walk through the library's doors. Whether a dabchick waddles or an old bird swoops in, the library can help uplift anyone who is willing to take flight anew.

PART I

Cultivating Ideas

1

What's the Idea, Plato?

When we are exalted by Ideas, we do not owe this to
Plato, but to the Idea, to which also Plato was debtor.

—RALPH WALDO EMERSON

Libraries are filled with ideas tucked away in books. Ideas may bubble up in a discussion program or a technology activity. Some ideas are "small" ones that can benefit us but have finite applications. Other ideas are "stupid" ones that don't benefit us and may even be harmful. We need to find and recognize the *big ideas*. What is a big idea? Some people may think it's like the genetic code of something, but that is not accurate. A big idea is not inherent in a physical form, nor can it be reproduced like the nucleotide base sequence of DNA. Although valuable, it is not the next marketing or branding opportunity. Likewise, a new educational curriculum on mathematics or a judicious operational approach for solar electric power may be important, but they do not translate into big ideas.

A big idea is what Plato referred to as an idea or pattern of thought stemming from a universal principle. Big ideas are blueprints for concepts that can help improve life. They embody the desire to make things better. Big ideas are designs of thinking for optimism (Helen Keller), freedom (Thomas Jefferson), charity for all (Abraham Lincoln), the examined life (Socrates), and energy (Nikola Tesla).

A way of understanding big, small, and stupid ideas is through understanding the big idea behind nourishment. The ancient Greek physician

Hippocrates realized that food enables a person's body and mind to help create vitality and maintain wellness. Often referred to as the "Father of Medicine," Hippocrates said, "Let thy food be thy medicine and thy medicine be thy food." The small idea of baking oatmeal-chocolate chip cookies can lead us to the blueprint of nourishment. By applying the recipe, cookies provide protein, iron, potassium, calcium, and vitamin A. Oatmeal-chocolate chip cookies for dessert or a snack offer both nutritional value and enjoyment. By contrast, a stupid idea would be an exclusive diet of cotton candy—which has no nutritional value. Although it may be a pleasant and satisfying experience, eating cotton candy three times a day doesn't connect to the big idea of nourishment as a way to create vitality and maintain wellness—and it may even cause harm to one's metabolism in the long run.

Where do big ideas come from, and how can libraries promote them? During the time of Plato, the Muses were said to have frolicked around the "Pierian springs" of northern Greece and would symbolically offer a cup of spring water—thereby transferring inspiration—to chosen philosophers, writers, and poets. Alexander Pope, the eighteenth-century English poet, wrote in his *Essay on Criticism* that "A little learning is a dang'rous thing; / Drink deep, or taste not the Pierian spring." The act of drinking the *full* cup of insight—delivered by the Muse—would be enough to inspire someone for a lifetime. Nikola Tesla, the brilliant electrical engineer, entrepreneur, and futurist, had a flash of understanding as a young adult about the fundamentals of electricity and spent the rest of his life trying to express all that he learned.

A common practice in ancient Greece was the *symposion* or "drinking party, a convivial gathering of the educated." It mixed relaxed conversation and creative discussion around big ideas. Tesla occasionally socialized with friends and associates over dinner for lively discussion. Julian Hawthorne, a friend of Tesla and son of Nathaniel Hawthorne, was struck by Tesla's abundance of culture. Rarely did one meet an engineer or scientist, Hawthorne noted, "who was also a poet, a philosopher, an appreciator of fine music, a linguist, and a connoisseur of food and drink."[1] All libraries should offer symposia—with or without drinking—but always with the enjoyment of discourse around big ideas.

Libraries have groups like book clubs where people state their opinions, but *stating an opinion is not thinking.* The origin of the word *opinion* can be traced to "conjecture," "fancy," "belief," "suppose," or "choose or prefer." By contrast, "truth" is "steadfast," and "knowledge" is "the capacity for learning and understanding." An opinion stems from a small idea that may be flawed by emotion or ambition. It may even be a stupid idea that is filled with bias and prejudice. Unfortunately, opinions are sometimes, and perhaps often, believed to be truth. Insights from great thinkers into defining why opinions are not true thinking include the following:

Opinion is the medium between knowledge and ignorance.
—PLATO

Prejudice is a great time saver.
You can form opinions without having to get the facts.
—E. B. WHITE

Science is the father of knowledge, but opinion breeds ignorance.
—HIPPOCRATES

Let me never fall into the vulgar mistake of dreaming
that I am persecuted whenever I am contradicted.
—RALPH WALDO EMERSON

Stubborn and ardent clinging to one's opinion
is the best proof of stupidity.
—MICHEL DE MONTAIGNE

It takes considerable knowledge just to realize
the extent of one's own ignorance.
—THOMAS SOWELL

Be able to notice all the confusion between fact
and opinion that appears in the news.
—MARILYN VOS SAVANT

Too often we enjoy the comfort of opinion
without the discomfort of thought.
—JOHN F. KENNEDY

A difference of opinion is what makes
horse racing and missionaries.
—WILL ROGERS

Most people are other people.
Their thoughts are someone else's opinions, their lives a mimicry.
—OSCAR WILDE

Loyalty to a petrified opinion never yet
broke a chain or freed a human soul.
—MARK TWAIN

The practice of thinking—inspired thinking or thinking things through—starts with discovering and examining big ideas.

Symposia are conversations open to all. They set the tone for thinking aloud with others rather than just debating or offering opinions. When stating an opinion based on what we've heard or read or believe we understand, the expression of bias becomes clear in the end result rather than genuine thinking. We may like an idea—the computer tablet—without understanding how it actually works or the big idea behind it (discovery). In a symposium, the goal is not to reach a consensus or persuade anybody to think differently. The objective is to explore the diverse ramifications of ideas—and the difference between big, small, and stupid ideas. In addition, these conversations encourage our appreciation of each other's company.

The big idea for libraries is to connect people to big ideas. A library of any type can do this—school, public, academic, and specialty libraries. A library of any size, budget, or staffing situation can do it.

It is astounding how little is taught about the distinction between big, small, and foolish or shortsighted ideas. A big idea may be the inspiration for a Shakespearean play—as the big idea of mercy is behind *The Merchant of Venice*—or the Harry Potter series. A big idea is the thought or true science behind electricity or robotics. A big idea can be a wellspring of insights that will improve scholarly research or generate a richer understanding of a poem or lead to the design for an alternating power system in a car engine between gas and electric power.

FIGURE 1.1

Shakespeare's *The Merchant of Venice* promotes the big idea of mercy. In Aaron Posner's reimagined version, *District Merchants,* Antonio (left), whose "pound of flesh" the moneylender Shylock (right) is after. The Folger Theatre, Washington, D.C.

Photograph with permission: Teresa Wood

Plato has challenged people for millennia. Instead of verifying a belief or opinion—small ideas—he sought the big ideas. He is credited with leading humanity on a quest for learning to use the mind. The superficiality of things has no place in big ideas. Plato coined the word *idea* (from Greek *idein*, "to see") to denote an immaterial pattern, archetype, or original universal concept. He explains that each person can train and exercise their mind to think and understand big ideas.

FIGURE 1.2

Plato (428/427–348/347 BC) was a philosopher in classical Greece and the founder of the Academy in Athens, the first institution of higher learning in the Western world.

Carol M. Highsmith, photographer. Main Reading Room. Portrait statue of Plato along the balustrade. Library of Congress, Thomas Jefferson Building, Washington, D.C. Washington D.C, 2007. Photograph. https://www.loc.gov/item/2007684417/.

Until a person, as described in Plato's dialogue *The Republic*, is able to rationally conceive of the idea of "the good," think through a gauntlet of objections, and judge things not in accordance with opinion but according to absolute truth, he does not yet know the idea of the good. If such a person "gets hold of some image [or imitation of the good], you'll say that it's through opinion, not knowledge."[2]

Plato describes an idea or pattern of thought stemming from a universal principle (big ideas) as something independent of individual thought (small ideas). Through the years, the distinction between opinion and knowledge, between small ideas and big ideas, has become distorted from Plato's original concept. In part, it was because the Greek word for "idea" has been translated into English as "form." A form refers to the physical shape of something or "the look of a thing," that is, a small idea. Plato was actually describing the ability "to see," understand, and express the universal concept, pattern, or essence behind something, a big idea.

Libraries of all types, sizes, and budgets are poised to tap the power of big ideas and strategically infuse them into their collection development, building design, customer services, and program planning. For example, as libraries serving young children create "play and learn centers," staffers can ponder the purpose of play in the library (a small idea). Librarians can further connect to the essence of creativity (a big idea) to lead to the love of learning (a big idea) to guide the design of library spaces.

Many libraries offer activities to engage youth and young adults through technology innovation labs and hands-on makerspaces. The big idea behind this type of service is flooding one's mind with curiosity and discovery. The participants may not realize they are investigating their potential, creating new opportunities for themselves, and learning marketable skills because they are immersed in the enjoyment of the activity. From virtual reality and robotics to creative writing classes and Shakespearean discussions to collaborative art projects, libraries can inspire curiosity, growth, and serving one's community.

John Couch, the author of *Rewiring Education: How Technology Can Unlock Every Student's Potential* and the vice president of education for Apple Inc., says that the excitement of learning in elementary school shifted to drudgery in middle and high school when he was growing up. "Explorations had been replaced by expectations, collaborating by competing, discovering by memorizing. . . . [These shifts capture] the main weakness of our current educational system: a focus on *what* to think, rather than *how* to think."[3]

Students are sometimes encouraged to do research, but not as a stimulus for thinking. They are taught to look for and find an answer, but not to learn how to ask the right questions. How can students stimulate their creativity to solve problems? How can they expand their awareness and maturity in order to respond to challenges? How can they—and all of us—increase their ability to reason, organize, and prioritize? Students can discover their niche in life through big ideas, such as their capacity for innovation (in science, technology, engineering, math, art, or literature) or a keen awareness of their responsibility for pursuing their duties (in business, management, education, environment, government, family, friends), or the ability to promote kindness and unity (in all that we do).

As Robert Kennedy explained, "Some men see things as they are, and ask why. I dream of things that never were, and ask why not." Big ideas stimulate the interest of students and enrich their awareness of what is possible. Alexander Pope encourages young people to drink deep of the cup of inspiration:

A little learning is a dang'rous thing;

Drink deep, or taste not the Pierian spring:

There shallow draughts intoxicate the brain,

And drinking largely sobers us again.

Fir'd at first sight with what the Muse imparts,

In fearless youth we tempt the heights of arts,

While from the bounded level of our mind,

Short views we take, nor see the lengths behind,

But more advanc'd, behold with strange surprise

New, distant scenes of endless science rise![4]

Plato describes how to talk with students about tapping big ideas versus small ideas and the value of big ideas in chapter 10 of his *Laws* dialogue. He encourages the students to learn the skill of discernment and thinking things through. The goal is to think before acting and especially before *re*acting. The "Athenian" in the story demonstrates to his friend, Clinias, how to speak to a student on this topic:

Now then . . . you're still young, and as time goes on you'll come to adopt opinions diametrically opposed to those you hold now. Why not wait till later on to make up your mind about these important matters [of distinguishing big ideas from small ideas]? The most important of all, however lightly you take it at the moment, is to get the right ideas about . . . [living] a good life:—*otherwise you'll live a bad one.* . . . [Y]ou're not unique. Neither you nor your friends are the first to have held this opinion . . . [that is, small idea thinking. You'll learn to tap big ideas and put them into action by discerning and gathering] your information from all sources . . . and then see which theory represents the truth.[5]

The real treasure in a library is the opportunity to access big ideas. The ultimate big idea is what Plato refers to as "the good." His message is: understanding how to live a good life is accomplished through working with big ideas. "Otherwise, you'll live a bad one."

Truly inspired human thinking always has its roots in a universal principle—in big ideas. Libraries can support and encourage big idea thinking in all areas of life, from education and government to business and the environment. Alexander Pope explored the big idea behind criticism, for example, to discover that it is not helpful to tear down a work of art by only finding its flaws, but to advocate for the ideal. As Pope says

Good-nature and good-sense must ever join;

To err is human; to forgive, divine.

In this way, the critic develops a habit or innate capacity not to ignore the flaws, but to recognize the blueprint or genius within a piece. The critic learns to judge not only the parts, but to focus on the whole. He or she approaches an examination of something in a balanced way—not too harsh, not too lenient. The result is to support and promote good art.

The ability to evaluate art or business or anything else in a useful way—a big idea way—means first learning to create and to think. It means developing a mental approach along with a guide to thinking clearly. It helps people of all ages and walks of life to work with big ideas and distinguish them from small idea criticism. The critic has a cherished duty—even more than the artist or poet or business person—to truth. The role of the critic is to consume the art or recite the poem or read a business report—and look for the big idea. The role is not to wallow in the imperfections of the piece, but to admire the inspiration behind it. Big idea criticism is not about frivolous admiration, motivation, or jealousy. It's about discerning the inner essence of meaning and developing our ability to write and speak about it.

Pope's *Essay on Criticism* exemplifies the ability to use big ideas to lift up the reader and encourage clear thinking. Written in a straightforward and conversational style, this nearly 6,000-word poem offers insights that are as relevant today as in 1711. Pope's acumen is refreshing as we grapple with modern challenges such as fabricated news, deceptive advertising, and the acceptance of lying as a political necessity.

The role of the library is to help people distinguish big ideas from small ideas (which are often practical and useful but not powerful) and from short-sighted or stupid ideas (which can be harmful) in order to tap those big ideas. Fortunately, it is relatively easy to do this. Great thinkers from Plato and Socrates onward have provided guidance. It involves learning not to dwell on imperfections. Playing "devil's advocate" is an invaluable aspect to examining projects and services—as long as it's accompanied by excellent planning. Successful libraries reach out and ask what people want. The best of human thinking and our ability to bring out the best in each other lies in our being able to explore, interact with, and be inspired by big ideas. Successful libraries of the future are helping their constituents to find, enumerate, and express big ideas.

To play off Walt Whitman:

> Come said the Muse,
> Read me a book no librarian has yet found,
> Read me the universal.
>
> In this new library,
> Amid the uninspiring and the slag,
> Enclosed and safe within its central heart,
> Nestles the seed perfection.
>
> By every curiosity more or less,
> Creativity born, conceal'd or unconceal'd
> The spark is waiting.

NOTES

1. Margaret Cheney, *Tesla: Man Out of Time* (1981; New York: Simon & Schuster, 2001), 109.

2. Plato, *Plato: Complete Works*, ed. John M. Cooper (Indianapolis, IN: Hackett, 1997), 1149.

3. John D. Couch and Jason Towne, *Rewiring Education: How Technology Can Unlock Every Student's Potential* (Dallas: Benbella Books, 2018), 2–4.

4. Alexander Pope, *An Essay on Criticism*, Poetry Foundation, https://www .poetryfoundation.org/articles/69379/an-essay-on-criticism.

5. Plato, *Plato: Complete Works*, 1545.

2

The Value of an Open Mind

We hold these truths to be self-evident . . .
—THOMAS JEFFERSON

Lynn J. Good, considered one of the most influential women leaders as the CEO of Duke Energy, a Fortune 500 company, says, "If you keep an open mind, you can learn so much from the people around you." A library can be a cornerstone for encouraging an open mind and has been at the heart of American education and culture for more than 250 years.

Cultivating an open mind lays the foundation for interacting with big ideas. It is better to have an open mind than a closed mind. People with a closed mind may not recognize big ideas and can miss using them to enrich their life, work, and talents. Inspired creativity thrives on an open mind combined with an ability to discern. An open mind without discernment may be more like a colander or sieve, where thinking is "riddled with holes." By learning the art of discernment, one can recognize—and tolerate—foolish or harmful ideas, but not accept or use them.

A library's visitors—and staffers—may believe they have an open mind because they employ a "nonjudgmental" approach to a situation. However, the mind is designed to judge in a thoughtful way—to be discerning. A judgment does not have to have an emotional charge. If it does, it is likely to be bigoted or biased. A judgment can avoid forming likes and dislikes, but instead be objective. The thinking mind can pass judgment using wisdom, maturity, and dignity. Library work today lends itself to activate and practice the skill of discernment, or the ability to think things through completely.

FIGURE 2.1

Opening minds and learning from those around you with Bubbler Makerspace programming. A former University of Wisconsin at Madison doctoral student, Will Porter, works with the Bubbler to engage Madison homeless and at-risk teenagers in an introductory course on the history of brass instruments around the world, followed by a hands-on lesson that culminates in the full group playing a simple tune together.

Photograph: Courtesy of Madison (WI) Public Library

Madison (WI) Public Library staffers take their popular "Bubbler" makerspace programming into community settings, helping to expand opportunities for creativity and open mind thinking. *Bubbler* is Wisconsin slang for a drinking fountain and is reminiscent of the idea of the ancient Greeks' Pierian spring of big ideas.

In order to successfully serve and engage people, librarians are learning to judge—to discern—using respect, acceptance, and grace. They become a model for others to train, nurture, and apply the mind. *Without* discernment, people are not able to find the best solutions. *With* discernment, people can disagree on issues yet entertain big ideas in order to meet challenges and move forward in life.

Inspired thinking and a can-do attitude are the results of an open mind using discernment. It doesn't matter whether the person standing in front of us in the library is young or old, with or without connections, or grew up under favorable circumstances or not; everyone has the ability to discover their talents, learn to develop their skills, and use courage to express their gifts. Success of this kind is always motivating because it teaches each of us that we can do it too. As Abraham Lincoln said, "Whatever you are, be a good one." A powerful resource for developing the open mind is the library.

The Library of Congress, the research library for the U.S. Congress, serves as a de facto national library. Congress appropriated $5,000 in 1801 to purchase "such books as may be necessary for the use of Congress," thus establishing the Library of Congress. Its 3,000 volumes were destroyed in a fire during the War of 1812. Former president Thomas Jefferson sold his personal library—the largest and finest library (public or private) in the United States at that time—to Congress in order to "recommence" the library with 6,487 volumes. Today, the Library of Congress is the world's largest library collection and contains tens of millions of books, photographs, newspapers, recordings, maps, and manuscripts.

It would surprise some people that Thomas Jefferson had an open mind attuned to the big ideas encountered in his day—and in our day. Even though he owned slaves—he lived in a society where slavery was accepted—he was instrumental in laying the groundwork that eventually ended slavery. Those who condemn Jefferson based on modern attitudes about slavery are demonstrating that they have a closed mind. A truly open mind accepts Jefferson as he was, not as we believe he ought to have been.

Jefferson witnessed the suppression of human freedoms and innovation, the worst excesses of monarchical governments, and the blight of civilization. Prior to the Revolutionary War he helped establish committees of correspondence to strengthen intercolonial bonds. His essays built his reputation for "literature, science, and a happy talent of composition," establishing him as a core team member and the lead author of the Declaration of Independence.

Jefferson devoted his life to the establishment of a country in which the innate human spirit of men and women was recognized. The freedom of individuals to grow intellectually, economically, and creatively was a big idea that was not yet fully established at that time, but it became the central theme for the new nation. Jefferson became the bridge between the lack of freedom for some and eventual freedom for all by declaring that "all men are created equal," meaning all human beings. It cannot be overstated how radical this idea—this big idea—was at the time. Thousands of people died during the American Revolution in the 1770s and the Civil War in the 1860s, bringing this big idea of freedom into human culture and civilization. Up until that time, the human spirit had been suppressed through destructive and degrading structures, such as slavery and hereditary aristocracies.

A library—with the purpose to enlighten humanity—extends the work begun by Jefferson. In a letter to John Adams in 1816, Jefferson wrote: "But ours will be the follies of enthusiasm, not of bigotry . . . the disease of ignorance, of morbid minds . . . Education and free discussion are the antidotes of both. We are destined to be a barrier against the returns of ignorance and barbarism. . . . What a stand will it secure as a ralliance for the reason and freedom of the globe! I like the dreams of the future better than the history of the past, —so good night! I will dream on, always fancying that Mrs. Adams and yourself are by my side marking the progress and the obliquities of ages and countries."[1] Librarians create an environment in which the innate human spirit of each person is recognized, nurtured, and celebrated.

Jefferson and others demonstrated the fullest degree of commitment to the concept or big idea of freedom for all—and were willing to pledge their lives to it. As Benjamin Franklin said after signing the Declaration of Independence, "We must indeed all hang together or, most assuredly, we shall hang separately."

The American colonies honored the ideal of freedom—both private and public—and stayed unified throughout the Revolution. But it took another eighty years for the United States to create a strong enough foundation to deal with the glaring hypocrisy of that ideal. Although a bitter Civil War ensued, the end result was a new level of unity among the states, the liberation of the slaves, and the partial implementation of Lincoln's idea—the big idea—of "malice toward none, with charity for all." With Lincoln's assassination before his plan for reconstruction could be fully realized, the application of charity for all took longer, but in time the country became far more united than divided. These gifts of freedom and charity of spirit have been passed down through the years.

Libraries have played—and continue to play—a key role in honoring the potential that each life in a free society represents. Who can better demonstrate how to honor all perspectives and efforts than a librarian? Who else—if not a librarian—is able to facilitate "free discussion" among a group of diverse individuals who can find common ground amid differing opinions? Who can share the big idea of freedom and help unify disparate factions more than a staffer in any library—school, university, public, or specialty library? No one is as consistent, skilled, or inspiring!

A Forbes Online opinion piece entitled "Amazon Should Replace Local Libraries to Save Taxpayers Money" serves as a creative wake-up call for libraries to focus on what we do best—share and promote big ideas. The library cannot be replaced. Another entity—with or without "prime" service—may be able to offer books for sale or on loan, but it cannot replace the advancement of big ideas. Despite the challenge from outside the library field—and the laments from inside the profession—questioning whether society needs libraries, people are responding favorably. EveryLibrary, a nonprofit advocacy group, and *Library Journal* magazine followed 133 library ballot measures in the United States in 2017, showing an amazing 90 percent pass rate.

It is up to each library to set in motion its ability to inspire open-mindedness and to encourage how to contemplate and implement big ideas. With an open mind, the possibilities are unlimited. In this way, a library of any type can help individuals, entrepreneurs, and students learn, grow, and flourish. They, in turn, will more than likely vote to support the library. By promoting big ideas, libraries nourish an ability to advance our understanding of science, technology, business, cultural arts, compassion, and fairness.

NOTE

1. Adrienne Koch and William Peden, eds., *The Life and Selected Writings of Thomas Jefferson* (New York: Modern Library, 2004), 618.

3

The Civilizing Force of Culture

When we want culture more than potatoes, and illumination more than sugar-plums, then the great resources of a world are . . . heroes, saints, poets, philosophers, and redeemers.

—HENRY DAVID THOREAU

No political bickerings or balderdash?

No rudeness?

Short, effective discussions?

No greed, exploitation, or antagonism?

No selfish opportunists?

Neighbors who are always considerate, tactful, and tolerant?

Intelligent cooperation where everyone is working in harmony
    for the common good?

Is this scenario too good to be true? Perhaps, but it's what we as human beings can aspire to achieving—in our work, family, and community—and in so doing can help create a civilizing force of culture. Problems and challenges can become unanticipated opportunities that bring out the best within people.

What function does the library play in civilization? What, in fact, is civilization? Is it a force that refines human awareness? Can libraries of all types stay out of politics and instead foster a climate that encourages the ability to think creatively and maturely, the skill to discover and apply intelligent change, and the know-how to promote the concepts of goodwill, forgiveness, tolerance, fairness, cooperation, and being a good neighbor?

The big idea of civilization is not reserved to any one country or continent. It did not begin in America with the Declaration of Independence or with the Renaissance in Europe. Civilization did not begin with the Great Library of Alexandria in Egypt, though, for a period of time, that library played a significant role by serving as the first major depository of universal writings from "all nations" for scholarly research.

We can trace civilization into the distant—most ancient—past and throughout the world. Humans have strived for many generations to develop skills to understand life, become their best, and contribute to life. The similarities of ancient mythologies among many cultures, for example, show evidence of the human effort throughout history to focus on helpfulness, courage, and wisdom. The stories of mythological gods and heroes have inspired human creativity from antiquity to the present.

Library programs and collections can help bring mythology to life as a keystone to human culture. The Library of Congress, for example, has over 160 subject headings under "Greek mythology."

Through her library's blog, Jennifer Thompson, the studio services librarian at Richland Library, South Carolina, encourages customers to explore mythology through books, movies, and other media: "There can be no doubt about *Star Wars* fanaticism, and with good reason—with a blend of Science Fiction and Western genres and a borrowing of tried and true mythology à la Joseph Campbell, it has something for (most) everyone. Even if you aren't a fan, you can still enjoy the works that influenced the franchise and if you are, *May the Force Be Ever in Your Favor, Mr. Potter*—Gandalf" in *The Chronicles of Narnia*.[1]

The University of Chicago Press offers more than sixty books related to mythology, with one title, *Folktales of India*, emphasizing "universal human characteristics—truthfulness, modesty, loyalty, courage, generosity, and honesty."[2]

The librarian Julie Smith and the instructional assistant Crystal Becker at Northampton (PA) Middle School created an online resource for students to easily link to recommended websites for exploring and studying Greek mythology. They encourage students to discover the contributions of mythology to the human story through the stories of Greek gods, goddesses, heroes, kings, and monsters.[3]

The slogan for the national Collaborative Summer Library Program (CSLP) in 2020 celebrates "Imagine Your Story" with subthemes: fairy tales, mythology, and fantasy.

FIGURE 3.1

The Delaware County Library District in Ohio commissioned a local artist, Dale Johnson, to create a sculpture for the library's Reading Garden on the theme of "mythological creatures." This work, entitled "Mythology -or- On the Origin of Stories," features several characters, including Cyclops, the blacksmith of the Greek Titans. Johnson says the Cyclops is "bringing creativity to the world, hammering and forging through the veil that separates the gods from humans."

Photograph: With Permission from Old World Stone Carving

The Greek story of Heracles, or as he has been popularly known since Roman times, Hercules, demonstrates the value of laboring for the benefit of humankind, which brings out the best within us. King Eurystheus gave Hercules twelve dangerous and "impossible" tasks or labors. For example, the second of the "Twelve Labors" entailed Hercules battling a monster called the Hydra. This story delivers a message of seeking inspiration, self-control, and focus in order to overcome all odds to kill the Hydra. Libraries can help promote the Herculean message of transforming adversity into triumph.

The ancient Egyptians, Indians, Incas, and many others helped move humanity forward by refining human insight and awareness. Human beings began to rise above selfishness and look beyond the superficial differences that separate and isolate people. Mythological stories contributed to the important work of learning to think about and express big ideas, such as respect and goodwill.

Although it can be easy to focus gloomily on wars, unfairness, and human shortcomings, each person has the capacity to grow in intelligence and awareness and act creatively to develop skills, solve problems, and do their best to make a valuable contribution to life—like the heroes and heroines of mythology. The understanding and realization that we can nurture the seeds of greatness within each person are part of the uplifting force of culture—and part of a library's purpose. Libraries across the spectrum can celebrate big ideas and help advance the civilizing force of culture.

August Wilson, the Pulitzer Prize–winning playwright, was the son of an alcoholic white father and an African American mother and grew up in "the Harlem of Pittsburgh" in the 1940s and 1950s. He dropped out of tenth grade after a teacher accused him of plagiarism. Wilson worked at menial jobs over the next five years while using a neighborhood Carnegie library to devour books. He said, "I was able to read anything I wanted. . . . I more or less educated myself." His story is an example of how a library can help individuals get to the heart of connecting with the best in life—under any circumstances.

The Supreme Court justice Clarence Thomas lived in rural poverty during his early childhood in Georgia. At age seven, his mother gave him and his brother over to her parents to raise in Savannah in 1955. His grandfather's mantra was: "Old Man *Can't* is dead." One of the few leisure-time activities allowed were regular trips to the nearby Carnegie public library because the librarians "helped us learn." Thomas said, "I spent countless hours immersed in the seafaring adventures of Captain Horatio Hornblower, the gridiron exploits of Crazy Legs McBain, and the real-life triumphs of Bob Hayes, the world's fastest man; I also read about the civil rights movement. . . . I was never prouder than when I got my first library card, though the day when I checked out enough books to fill it up came close."[4]

Civilization can provide a focus for anyone—who is interested, curious, and open-minded—to discover the great thinkers and learn from earlier times. It is a force that restores humanity again and again. *There are many agents or*

potential channels for developing civilization and advancing human achievement.
A well-stocked library—with books, learning activities, and inspired staff—is one.
Although a library cannot do the work of civilization by itself, it can play an
important part.

Even a small library provides access to great literature to improve understanding. It helps people discover art and music to refine perceptions. The
library—academic, public, specialty, or school—encourages people to think,
learn, and grow. A top-notch library plays an important role as a civilizing
influence within a city, a school, or a college campus. It develops culture and
civilization where excellent friendships cultivate the capacity to respect one
another. It meets individuals where they are to help them discover their
potential. For example, a good library can help a father learn to navigate the
legal system in order to successfully appeal his case on his own and obtain cus-
tody of his children. Librarians may not often know whether they make such
an impact, but what matters is that first-rate service is offered. Joan Bellis-
tri, law library director at the Anne Arundel County (MD) Public Law Library,
says, "Sometimes people come back saying that we may not remember them,
but letting us know that their situation worked out well."

In tracing the significance of libraries in civilization and human history,
we find that they have helped promote the power of individual genius and
accomplishment. They played a quiet, but important role. Some private libraries during the European Renaissance were open to the public, encouraging
the exchange of big ideas, reading, and scholarship. Libraries—public, private,
and scholarly—were instrumental in early America, making available the big
ideas that helped shape the thinking and understanding that led to freedom
from England. Abolitionist pamphlets and broadsides, such as those of William
Lloyd Garrison (founder of the Abolitionist Anti-Slavery Society), Theodore
Parker, Wendell Phillips, and others, helped convey ideas to end the institution of slavery. Many of those abolitionist publications were donated to the
Boston Public Library in 1895.

The Allegheny County Law Library in Pittsburgh, Pennsylvania, established in 1867—once the largest law library in the world—is a public law
library that is open to legal professionals and the general public free of charge.
Entering the Beaux Arts-style "city hall" building housing the library—with
its arched windows and grand entrances and staircases—inspires strength,
authority, and grace. The law library's reading room is like a magnet drawing
us in and inviting us to access its great wealth of resources.

Another example of cultivating civilization in action is the Mercantile
Library of Cincinnati. Since its founding in 1835, it has served as a cultural
center. Those who established the Mercantile Library may have been fueled
by the witty commentary of Mrs. Frances Trollope, an English travel writer
(and mother of the novelist Anthony Trollope), who wrote two volumes about
her travels in America from 1827 to 1831. Reading her work shows that she
was looking for utopia and did not connect the dots that America was a work

in progress. Mark Twain said, "Mrs. Trollope was so handsomely cursed and reviled by this nation [for] telling the truth. . . . She was painting a state of things which did not disappear at once. . . . I remember it. . . . She found a 'civilization' here which you, reader, could not have endured; and which you would not have regarded as a civilization at all. [She spoke] in plain terms . . . but honest and without malice. . . . She deserved gratitude. . . . She did not gild us; and neither did she whitewash us."[5]

FIGURE 3.2

Members and visitors peruse items at the Mercantile Library in downtown Cincinnati while awaiting a noontime concert.

Rick Dikeman (public domain)

Culture can be defined as that which helps individuals shine through the improvement of the mind, such as developing the skills to be genuine, conscientious, mature, thoughtful, and cheerful. Cincinnati's Mercantile Library founders banded together for self-improvement and said: "Let us grasp at every means of improvement within our reach; let us read, think, act, in the living present; let us strive earnestly and heartily for that dignified and ennobling self-culture, to which every end, and aim, and object of life shall converge as toward a common center—without which man is of little worth, and with which he can accomplish all things."[6]

As Cincinnati grew from a village to a city of "unlimited promise" and was fondly referred to by Henry Wadsworth Longfellow as the "Queen of the West," the Mercantile Library played its part in promoting culture, including offering a lecture series. The lecture series thrived by featuring local, national, and international speakers such as Ralph Waldo Emerson, William Makepeace

Thackeray, Herman Melville, and Harriet Beecher Stowe. This tradition continues with the annual Niehoff Lectures, which have hosted speakers and writers such as John Updike, Tom Wolfe, Ray Bradbury, Julia Child, and Jonathan Winters. There are also other types of events, small concerts, and learning activities that are often scheduled at lunchtime for the convenience of the city's downtown population.

The Allegheny County (Pittsburgh) Law Library, the Mercantile Library of Cincinnati, Richland (SC) Library, Boston Public Library, Maryland State Law Library, Northampton (PA) Middle School Library, Anne Arundel (MD) Public Law Library, the Library of Congress, Carnegie libraries across the country, and other libraries across the spectrum offer tools, knowledge, and ability to explore an idea and understand the truth in each case or circumstance. Staffers can afford an opportunity for their patrons and students to discover the big idea behind any situation at hand and can prompt the best solutions.

Library staff members at all levels have a great opportunity to build a bridge between clients or students and big ideas. As this does not happen a lot, we must ask ourselves: Does the library encourage a culture of destructive gossip—or inspiring conversations? Does it promote a culture of corruption—or humanitarian works and programs to enrich life? Catherine McGuire, director of the Maryland State Law Library, starts with the basic question: what can we do to help? "When someone from the general public shows an interest, we strive to show them how the law fits into their lives so they are more informed and have the ability to help themselves," says McGuire.

Libraries are a work in progress. They continually provide a portal for civilization. Cincinnati in 1830 was pretty rough and ready, but now the city is an example of an ever-expanding and creative community. The libraries in Cincinnati—specialty, public, academic, and school—have played a quiet but important role. This is true in every city, town, and neighborhood. Libraries are growing into what may be their most impactful role—to build a bridge to big ideas.

NOTES

1. Richland Library, https://www.richlandlibrary.com/recommend/your -obligatory-star-wars-post.
2. University of Chicago Press, https://www.press.uchicago.edu/ucp/books/book/ chicago/F/bo5375414.html.
3. Northampton Middle School Library Media Center Website, https:/sites .google.com/a/nasdschools.org/middle-school-library/english/greek-gods-and -goddesses.
4. Clarence Thomas, *My Grandfather's Son: A Memoir* (New York: Harper, 2007), 17.
5. Frances Trollope, *Domestic Manners of the Americans* (originally published London, 1832); also "edited with a history of Mrs. Trollope's Adventures in America," ed. Donald Smalley (New York: Vintage, 1949).
6. Robert C. Vitz, *At the Center: 175 Years at Cincinnati's Mercantile Library* (Cincinnati, OH: Mercantile Library, 2010), 6–7.

PART II

Building Bridges to Big Ideas

4

Designing a Blueprint

A fo ben, bid bont.
Translation: If you want to be a leader, be a bridge.

—WELSH PROVERB

Whether it is a beam, arch, or a truss bridge, engineers have been building bridges since ancient times. Whether it is a bridge across a large river or one that makes it possible to stroll across a chasm in the landscape, bridge-building is both practical and aesthetic. Bridges can be found throughout the world carrying cars, trains, cyclists, and pedestrians. There is even a technology process called a "bridge library" that can help facilitate communication within electronic platforms.

How many bridges can be found in the library? Can you think of some bridges that don't exist but could? Design insights and information on bridge-building can be discovered in books on civil engineering, architecture, and construction, of course, but also in using children's toys, such as Legos and Keva planks, and in STEM activities and library play-and-learn centers. Literal and figurative bridge-building are referenced in poetry, philosophy, fables, Shakespeare, leadership trainings, and trick-taking card games.

A bridge of trust and goodwill between people can strengthen a friendship, boost a project, raise a child, write a successful grant, or produce an effective firefighting team. Libraries can help build bridges between big ideas, such as truthfulness, patience, courage, and respect, and a person's ability to implement and express them. As people connect with the big idea of optimism, for example, they can generate cheerfulness, confidence, and kindness, creating new opportunities to contribute in life—even under difficult circumstances.

Unless libraries pay attention to their ability to help people connect with big ideas, they can miss their chance to make a meaningful impact. Do library staff spend too much time ruminating about what's wrong or missing in a situation? Can they free up time and energy to effectively connect with big ideas to better problem-solve and plan? Are library staffers developing skills to build their own personal and professional bridges to big ideas in order to help the individuals they serve do the same?

OUTLINING RIGHT EXPECTATIONS

The first bridge for we librarians to build is to make a commitment of our own to big ideas. The big ideas of ingenuity, honesty, generosity, wisdom, and joy have been around for a long time. Even college philosophy courses, such as an introduction to Plato, don't focus enough on them. We have a tendency to become lost in a forest of opinions, trends, and fads—which can lead to confusion and false information. We can miss the value-added nature of big ideas if we don't recognize their integrity.

Details are important, but not if they override what is essential in serving students, patrons, and customers. Chunking the work down into manageable parts helps keep the work moving at a steady pace for any type of community or group served. However, keeping a larger perspective is also required for library success.

Creating a blueprint or design for construction can help a library build a bridge to big ideas. Every bridge that can withstand the stresses of its function starts with blueprints and plans. An effective design will help organize the building process. A mental blueprint will give instructions and show how to sort out conflicting information.

The first and primary source for big ideas, for example, is classical literature, poetry, philosophy, and the arts. A library is an excellent place for people to search and connect with these resources. Emerging technologies, learning platforms, and the like are creating unprecedented opportunities for librarians to construct bridges to big ideas in new and effective ways.

No matter what learning tool is used, the need for a librarian to be curious, learn the right things, and think things through in order to offer compelling service remains the same. The big ideas of gratitude, beauty, love, achievement, selfhood, and dignity likewise remain constant. The goal is to help people connect with these concepts and discover ways to express them.

FIGURE 4.1

Building a bridge between history enthusiasts and the big idea of technology. A library traveling exhibit on tour, featuring augmented reality to bring local history to life. A collaboration among Union Mills Homestead, BaltiVirtual, and Carroll County (MD) Public Library.

Photograph: Courtesy of Carroll County (MD) Public Library

Misinformation can result if the right inspiration is not sought. Confusion is created when we don't know how to look for big ideas or don't know where to find them.

Traditionally, librarians have embraced the roles of information organizers, researchers, and guides to literature. We are successfully promoting the love of reading, and, increasingly, the enjoyment of lifelong learning. But have librarians encouraged the ability to think things through completely and thoroughly?

Busy modern lifestyles with their complexity of duties require us to think independently in order to be successful. How can libraries be a resource for learning to think in ways that add value to every situation, plan, or service? What books, activities, and services can be offered to discourage groupthink?

For example, if a young person automatically adopts a narrow interpretation about an issue based on peer influence or doing a quick online search, does the library promote a wider range of information, viewpoints, and

PLANNING FOR BIG IDEAS

A plan requires us to have the right expectations about how to find ideas and be able to distinguish big ideas from foolish ones. A blueprint for right expectations includes

- always learning more in any circumstance (whether successful or not);
- learning to think completely and thoroughly about an idea, situation, or event;
- speculating about accepted traditions and exploring their meaning and relevance, if any;
- testing the validity and usefulness of an idea in practical circumstances;
- recognizing that certain beliefs may have "unexpected consequences" before making a decision or taking action based on those beliefs;
- unlearning anxiety, arrogance, and stubbornness in order to make room to explore and develop our strengths;
- greeting ideas that may be potentially challenging or mysterious without fear or automatically assuming they won't be useful;
- increasing our sensitivity to big ideas by not being too passive, thereby closing our awareness;
- understanding the underlying purpose and meaning behind an idea
- observing the results of implementing an idea; and
- nurturing desired results instead of obsessing on eradicating what is not working.

opportunities for learning more? Matthew Reidsma, the web services librarian at Grand Valley State University in Michigan and the author of *Customizing Vendor Systems for Better User Experiences*, says: "We're about transforming people, and that involves access to information, but it also involves access to people, to community, to librarians, to other users. This is a different way of thinking about our work that is on a higher level than task-based thinking. We're thinking about the experience of the people involved, and what happens when they use the library."

Can a library help people of all ages, backgrounds, and abilities develop the courage to think for themselves? Does the library challenge its patrons to think or merely prove a point? A key challenge is to determine how to find ideas and distinguish big ideas from foolish ones. By laying out a blueprint to build a bridge to big ideas, librarians can gain momentum to successfully grapple with these and other questions. Qualities that can help design a useful blueprint are the ability to unlearn coupled with the skill to nurture desired results.

UNLEARNING TO MAKE ROOM FOR THE NEW

John P. Kotter of the Harvard Business School says, "Never underestimate the magnitude of the power of the forces that reinforce the status quo." Whether it is a force within an individual to maintain the status quo or a force within an organization to create a follow-the-herd atmosphere, unlearning can help counter these and other barriers to growth. Unlearning is crucial in making room for new understanding and skills development. It taps our potential as lifelong learners. *Unlearning makes us independent thinkers because we have to skillfully and consistently reject a plethora of informational muck.*

If we have a tendency to view problems as threats, can we unlearn and thoughtfully examine them, instead, as opportunities? Yes! If we focus only on someone's overreaction in a discussion and miss the substance of the situation, can we unlearn and apply discernment in order to focus on how to be helpful? Yes! If we rely too much on the approval of others, can we unlearn in order to develop an entrepreneurial spirit to nurture the work on our own? Absolutely.

The online "Lessons Learned" website created by the Federal Aviation Administration captures safety information, actions, and improvements associated with the accidents of small airplanes, helicopters, and transport aircraft. For example, a helicopter collision with a red-tailed hawk resulted in industry unlearning, with recommendations for a redesign of the control system quadrant to help prevent unintended movement of the engine power control levers.

NURTURING DESIRED RESULTS

Many of us have a tendency to greet new ideas with doubt. Part of the problem is being in the habit of focusing on what is annoying instead of what's working. It is important to examine what's not working and what needs changing in order to be more effective, but not without paying attention to the many elements of success and fulfillment in life. By paying too much attention to our frustrations, we increase our sense of overall disappointment and risk missing opportunities to improve library service. If we pay attention to what is working and celebrate our strengths and accomplishments, we will create a momentum for future opportunities and continued achievement.

In 1988, the Watauga County (NC) Public Library carefully planned the opening of a new branch in combination with a community center and a project on aging. Part of the plan was to bridge the gap between generations. "We hope to work with senior citizens and children and have them volunteer together. There is a tendency to separate ages, and this is the ideal time to help them work together," said librarian Jackie Cornette. Celebrating thirty years of collaboration, the library and community center offer not only books and activities, but also new and emerging technology and digital resources. They put the big ideas of kindness, reverence, and gracefulness into action through socialization and volunteer opportunities.

Blueprints to build bridges to wisdom, harmony, beauty, and other big ideas are often created in the mind of leaders—and celebrated! They may or may not be written down. However, without a firm foundation of right expectations, the blueprint will be just an exercise in thinking and will not have the power of action. Whether in a small town, a university, a school, or online, the library can potentially play a central role in paving the way to build bridges to big ideas.

5

Building the Bridge

But which is the stone that supports the bridge?

—KUBLAI KHAN

The bridges that libraries are building to big ideas require strong building blocks. Library staffers need qualities and skills such as the purposeful use of thought, the compassionate use of authority, and the quiet use of joy in our work.

Generally, we librarians have been an orderly and stable type of professional group. Since the opening of Benjamin Franklin's public library in 1731, we have focused on rules to promote the return of books, the management of collections, oversight of information research, and serving individuals. Rules are important, but the most effective rules are those that derive from principles—trustworthiness, integrity, and hard work. Above and beyond the "rules," librarians are increasingly striving to inspire curiosity through many new approaches to learning, interaction, and creativity. Today's librarian is learning to embrace the overarching philosophy of Franklin and Andrew Carnegie: *to enlighten humanity*. The practical implementation of this philosophy is threefold: to advocate self-improvement by promoting maturity and seeking solutions, to encourage mindfulness and enable greater access to helpful insights and creative abilities, and to nourish self-reliance by developing skills.

Self-improvement, mindfulness, and self-reliance are the foundational materials for bridge-building to big ideas.

SELF-IMPROVEMENT

Emily Cabaniss, the librarian for the Seattle Opera company, manages reference questions backstage, oversees the archives, fields public requests, and performs other duties as assigned—such as coordinating the care of the company's musical instruments. Whether it is Mozart's *The Marriage of Figaro*, Verdi's *La Traviata*, or Wagner's *The Flying Dutchman*, Cabaniss describes opera as an "opportunity for people to explore concepts such as compassion, love, and redemption through music, singing and drama."

FIGURE 5.1

Opera helps promote the big ideas of beauty, nobility, and unity. Among her myriad responsibilities, the Seattle Opera librarian, Emily Cabaniss, checks whether it's time to oil a Wagner tuba.

Photograph: Courtesy of Seattle Opera

Demonstrating the power of opera to move and inspire, the Seattle Opera, New York Metropolitan Opera, Fort Worth Opera, Lyric Opera of Chicago, Maryland Opera, and many other companies across the country are flourishing—and not only among traditional audiences. According to Cabaniss, the Seattle Opera's young professionals group, BRAVO!, with members aged 21 to 39 years, has become the largest share of operagoers.

Any type or size of library can promote opera with or without an opera house. Librarians can introduce patrons to opera through music CDs, books, and programs or connect to archival and live productions of the Metropolitan Opera online, over the airwaves, or via satellite. Alexandra Day, the deputy vice-president for alumni engagement at Princeton University, adds that listening to opera can connect people to higher aspirations, greater empathy, and more profound self-knowledge. Day explains, "The experience of opera—on stage, in the movies, or through a podcast—is a way in which society can express the abstract truths about life above and beyond the material elements of culture."

MINDFULNESS

Joy "can be found, even in the darkest of times, if only one remembers to turn on the light," says the character Dumbledore in the Harry Potter movie *The Prisoner of Azkaban*. Mindfulness is foundational to building a bridge to big ideas like joy. It is the ability to think more clearly, entertain more realistic insights, and plan better strategies.

The first step to mindfulness is the skill of detachment, which recognizes that we each have abilities—if applied successfully—to be a problem-solver in any circumstance. Detachment focuses our attention so that we can stay above the fray of emotions and handle difficulties with a bit more grace and composure. It can facilitate our ability to enjoy life despite ongoing challenges and without denying the struggles of life. We learn to be less distracted by problems, knowing that we have what it takes to resolve them.

"By getting staff at all levels to think about the bigger picture, we can design better services and library spaces. We can apply trial and error and turn mistakes into great learning to improve user experience," says Lucy Holman, university librarian at the University of North Carolina–Wilmington. The goal is to get into the habit of paying attention to the best in ourselves and others. We can help develop the know-how to produce worthwhile results by expanding the skill of thinking things through. By focusing energy on our potential and growth, we can accelerate that growth exponentially.

Librarians can promote the difference between careless thinking and mindfulness through thoughtful poetry, inspiring plays, and lessons learned through fictional characters. For example, the William Andrews Clark Memorial Library at the University of California–Los Angeles houses a renowned collection of rare books and manuscripts from England's Tudor period through the eighteenth century. It includes the world's largest repository of materials related to the Irish author Oscar Wilde and a collection of the works of John Dryden, England's first poet laureate. Both Dryden and Wilde startled their contemporary societies by using humor and wit in poetry and playwriting to expose hypocrisy. They articulated what few were willing or able to express. They promoted mature mindfulness. Dryden's poem "The Secular Masque" said that his era was

> a quaffing and unthinking time. . . .
> 'Tis well an old age is out, and time to begin anew.

Many volumes of these rare books and manuscripts are digitized and available online, where anyone can discover big ideas to tap, ponder, and apply.

Mindfulness helps us disentangle unresolved conflicts that can distract us from making useful decisions. Mindfulness is not emotionally based; it fills the mind with inspiration that nurtures the best within us and embraces the wholeness of life. Mindfulness restores our ability to think thoroughly and completely. It keeps us focused on connecting with big ideas, such as creativity, wisdom, forgiveness, self-control, endurance, and courage, and enables us to act on these concepts and rely on them time and again.

SELF-RELIANCE

It's easy to adopt a crowd outlook—and, even worse, a mass of emotional prejudices. However, some librarians demonstrate an effective antidote to groupthink by, in effect, minding their own business when offering services by guiding, not telling, people what to do and what not to do. They treat people with respect and goodwill—big ideas in action—and encourage people to develop their potential by exploring resources, trying new activities, and enjoying the process.

Discovering—and cultivating—human potential can seem a little vague. What does it mean, after all? The intention is to unveil or draw out what Plato called "the good" in others. Benjamin Franklin described being your best in order to "work for the common good." Abraham Lincoln stated, "Whatever you are, be a good one."

With a nod or two to Charles Dickens, libraries exist today in "the best of times and the worst of times." While many people know that libraries offer workforce resources to benefit their community, for example, those in need of job information may not be aware of specific services at their local library. It can simultaneously be the spring of hope and the winter of despair if a library serves a dozen young adults each day who are not working and not in school—but it doesn't have a plan to serve them wisely.

Ralph Waldo Emerson, the nineteenth-century American essayist, lec-turer, and poet, demonstrated a pragmatic approach to helping people become their best selves and always be lifelong learners. His essay on "Self-Reliance" is a guide to thinking things through. In it, Emerson reminds us that a human being is designed to be his or her best in life, like a rose. The rosebud develops and grows into what it is meant to be in life, a beautiful, perfect flower. How can a library help a person draw forth their talent?

Emerson's series of essays on topics such as experience and friendship, as well as self-reliance, offer a treasure trove of ideas for librarians to pon-der, absorb, and apply to workforce and business development services. He encourages each person to learn to think for herself, in order not to be swayed by popular opinion or groupthink.

In some schools, children are given an assignment to copy a text word-for-word and then are praised for their ability "to write" an essay. By the time they reach middle and high school, these students cannot easily discern between an opinion and original thinking. Emerson promotes the big idea of self-re-liance and asserts that one's "conformity explains nothing." Each person can "know that power is inborn, that he is weak because he has looked for good out of him and elsewhere, and so perceiving, throws himself unhesitatingly on his thought, instantly rights himself, stands in the erect position, commands his limbs, and can work miracles."

FIGURE 5.2

The Enoch Pratt Free Library's mobile job center visits communities in Baltimore to provide support where access to services can be challenging.

Photograph: Courtesy of Enoch Pratt Free Library

Depending on the community, a library may take on an employment agency-like role, but libraries are not employment agencies. Libraries can sup-port the work of employment resource centers through satellite job centers. They can help entrepreneurs start a business through their makerspaces or career and business centers. However, a library's ability to design a culture of learning and an environment of exploration is a crucial ingredient for thriving library service.

FIGURE 5.3

Celebrating their ninth anniversary in fall 2017, the owners of The Palette & The Page started their business using the Cecil County (MD) Public Library's Small Business Information Center. (Left to right: Lynn Whitt, Patti Paulus, and Janet Youse.)

Photograph: Courtesy of The Palette & The Page

Developing the habit of thinking ideas through will help people learn skills, make wise decisions, and expand opportunities. How can the process of offering resources, activities, and support to students, entrepreneurs, and out-of-work individuals help them explore their potential, develop intelligent risk-taking skills, and in effect, become their best selves? To quote Emerson on self-reliance once more, "Be real and admirable, not as we know, but as you know. Able men do not care in what kind a man is able, so only that he is able. A master likes a master, and does not stipulate whether it be orator, artist, craftsman, or king."

Self-improvement, mindfulness, and self-reliance are implementation strategies to help libraries "enlighten humanity" and build a bridge to big ideas. Libraries that are transforming and thriving don't just pay lip service to the qualities of joy, courage, and perseverance. Research suggests that intangible assets drive the creation of economic value and along with this, provide new ways for libraries to measure and communicate their value. *Many libraries—public, academic, school, and specialty—are successful because they offer something beyond anyone else's capabilities.*

6

Using the Bridge to Enlightenment

I would rather be the man who bought the Brooklyn Bridge than the man who sold it. —WILL ROGERS

Wayne Bivens-Tatum, the philosophy and religion librarian at the Princeton University Library, says that enlightenment "means to illuminate metaphorically, to direct light onto something, usually with the purpose to understand the thing"—or at a higher level—the idea.[1] As librarians, we have an important obligation to explore the big ideas of contentment, peace, and goodwill and provide access to them for our patrons, students, and customers. When we cross the bridge to the big ideas of curiosity, empathy, and joy, for example, we are taking a leap into the realm of applying curiosity in fresh ways, understanding the unlimited potential of empathy, and expressing joy to enrich life, especially during extensive challenges.

Librarians are sitting on a treasure trove of big ideas, wisdom, awareness, and insights in the stacks, physical and virtual, and in their offerings of activities. Can we help an individual, young or old, discover poetry that has stood the test of time from the pen of William Shakespeare, Elizabeth Barrett Browning, or Alexander Pope? For example, how can pondering the following short poem, based on an Aesop fable, inspire us to think things through and tap maturity and objectivity?

A jar of honey chanced to spill

Its contents on the windowsill

In many a viscous pool and rill.

The flies, attracted by the sweet,

Began so greedily to eat,

They smeared their fragile wings and feet.

With many a twitch and pull in vain

They gasped to get away again,

And died in aromatic pain.

O foolish creatures that destroy

Themselves for transitory joy.

Can reading a "forbidden" tome, such as Nathaniel Hawthorne's *The Scarlet Letter*, Mark Twain's *The Adventures of Huckleberry Finn*, or Madeleine L'Engle's *A Wrinkle in Time*, influence a library visitor to explore a big idea or two? Banned books may be forbidden by some, but almost always they have stood the test of time.

According to the ALA's Office for Intellectual Freedom, Twain's story of Huck and his friend Jim rafting down the Mississippi River, first published in 1885, was instantly rejected by some for its coarseness. For example, using the words "sweat" instead of perspiration and "itched" instead of scratched was considered crude and inelegant. In recent decades, the book has been rejected for Twain's nineteenth-century racial language. But despite its being one of the most challenged books, *The Adventures of Huckleberry Finn* retains its power and readership because it offers insights into the values of respect, friendship, and honesty, as well as exploring the big ideas of freedom, nobility, and wisdom.

The big idea of freedom does not give us carte blanche to misbehave. Freedom is not a state of being where you are free to do whatever you want or impose on others. Freedom liberates the mind. The meaning of "freedom," derived from the Old English word *freodom*, is the power of self-determination. The function of freedom is love, dignity, and joy.

Instead of offering a pedagogical approach to learning, libraries can champion programs and services in ways that promote "freedom" and liberate the mind. For example, libraries are grappling with how to support customers in using new and emerging technology. Working with librarians on this effort, Lisa Guernsey, the director of learning technologies at the New America think tank, says, "Librarians help give people a framework for making their own decisions. They don't offer rules of what to do or not do, but encourage families to consider the content, context, and an individual child's interests and potential for learning." Librarians encourage each person, family, or business to make their own wise decisions about technology. In these ways, students, clients, and patrons are figuring out what they know and can do in order to be their best in whatever they try. Whether it's with technology or literature or poetry, librarians strive to promote freedom and liberate minds by sparking curiosity, courage, and creativity.

The characters Meg and her friend Calvin in *A Wrinkle in Time* try to understand the lyrics from the beautiful music of the garden creatures. With the help of Mrs. Whatsit, they discover that the singing doesn't translate into words, per se, but is experienced as joy flowing "through them, back and forth between them, around them and about them and inside them." Although L'Engle's *A Wrinkle in Time* (1962) won the Newbery Award for best children's book, it is a book to be enjoyed by all ages. The story combines aspects of science fiction, fantasy, and realistic fiction to tell a tale of love and truth winning out over misfortune and hatred. It was praised by many, yet it was banned by some churches, schools, and libraries.

A Wrinkle in Time has continued to be challenged and even banned nearly every year for one of two primary reasons—either for being too religious or for undermining religion. L'Engle summed up the controversy: "We find what we are looking for. If we are looking for life and love and openness and growth, we are likely to find them. If we are looking for witchcraft and evil, we'll likely find them, and we may get taken over by them."[2]

Barriers to Thinking Big

Several factors can hinder or even prevent a librarian's ability to use the bridge to enlightenment or big ideas effectively in order to connect them to her community or constituency:

1. A common practice is to default to "dumbing down" big ideas. We may treat joy as mere happiness, for example. We may apply our own concepts to ideas instead of pursuing what big ideas are and can do.

2. Some of us have a tendency to fixate on what is wrong about life and disregard what is working well. Library staff members may miss an opportunity to boost a collaborative project, or they may obsess about a mistake made by a colleague or by themselves.

3. We may focus on work conditions or budget circumstances or other people's behavior as a primary source of problems. As a result, we stop paying attention to what we can control—our own attitudes, intentions, and actions. If a colleague is having a bad day and says something unkind, we may allow ourselves to become upset, miss a deadline, and blame that person.

(Cont.)

4. Instead of dwelling on past losses or mistakes, we must free up energy to activate mature thinking, confidence, and hope. For example, a department head recovers from a gloomy decision outlook after losing a position and develops a renewed ability to use humor to increase her creativity and productivity despite the loss.

5. Assumptions such as "life is not fair" can cripple our ability to cross the bridge to enlightenment. We need to apply courage and integrity by asking ourselves whether a disappointment should be a permanent fixture in our mind or if it can be dissolved with contentment and common sense. A library director initially feels shattered when she gets word about severe budget cuts, but she taps the wisdom to plan and work from a center of strength and develops a series of insightful and proactive ways to transform the crisis into opportunity.

6. We may display a lack of curiosity about what lies beyond the ordinary.

When we remove barriers, it frees us up to develop strategies to use the bridge. It is important that the effort to cross the bridge should be led by the best within us. We cross the bridge to connect with big ideas.

TUNING INTO BIG IDEAS

Over a century ago, Helen Keller, an author and lecturer who was the first blind and deaf person to earn a college degree, wrote: "Once or twice I have wrestled with evil [harmful ideas], and for a time felt its chilling touch on my life; so I speak with knowledge when I say that evil is of no consequence, except as a sort of mental gymnastic. For the reason that I have come in contact with it, I am more truly an optimist. . . . It makes us strong, patient, helpful men and women. . . . My optimism, then, does not rest on the absence of evil, but in the preponderance of good and a willing effort always to cooperate with the good, that it may prevail."[3]

It doesn't matter what one's background, age, or circumstances are: a big idea—the good, as exalted by Plato—can give us new insight into any situation in which we find ourselves. A set of core values is a prerequisite to living as a successful individual and playing a role in a thriving organization. We can be so busy contributing to the operation of our libraries that we don't pause to reflect on core values. However, we may still have core values and honor them in order to create effective library services, programs, and collaborations. The key is to activate core values such as honesty, hard work, curiosity, helpfulness, cooperation, perseverance, discipline, patience, cheerfulness, and humor, plus the idea of treating others the way we'd like to be treated. These core values form the foundation for productive living and expand our ability to mobilize big ideas.

Great thinkers who have stood the test of time formed similar core values and knew how to tune into big ideas. Benjamin Franklin said of patience, "He that can have patience can have what he will." Other examples of great thinkers include Helen Keller, Sir Isaac Newton, Sir Francis Bacon, Thomas Jefferson, George Washington, Socrates, Plato, Hippocrates, Confucius, René Descartes, C. S. Lewis, Abraham Lincoln, Andrew Carnegie, Sir Winston Churchill, Albert Schweitzer, Paramahansa Yogananda, Albert Einstein, Maria Montessori, and Nikola Tesla.

Great English-speaking poets who have expressed big ideas such as oneness, wholeness, love, and peace include Alexander Pope, Elizabeth Barrett Browning, Robert Browning, John Masefield, John Keats, Robert Frost, and Henry Wadsworth Longfellow.

A sampling of not-to-be-missed writers would include William Shakespeare, Ralph Waldo Emerson, Nathaniel Hawthorne, Henry David Thoreau, Mark Twain, Sir Arthur Conan Doyle, Omar Khayyam, Hermann Hesse, Johann Wolfgang von Goethe, Rudyard Kipling, Saki, and William Somerset Maugham.

Artists bringing beauty and inspiration into the world include Monet, Nicholas Roerich, Thomas Cole, Salvador Dali, Rembrandt, Leonardo da Vinci, and Arthur Rackham.

Beethoven, Mozart, Handel, Bach, Haydn, Debussy, Holst, Wagner, Mendelssohn, Tchaikovsky, Vivaldi, Purandara Dasa, and Clara Schumann have ridden the wavelength of big ideas and brought joy, redemption, and triumph to humanity through their music.

Helen Keller wrote to the New York Symphony Orchestra in 1924 about her experience "listening" on the radio to their performance of Beethoven's Ninth Symphony as a deaf-blind person. "Last night, when the family was listening to your wonderful rendering of the immortal symphony, someone suggested that I put my hand on the receiver and see if I could get any of the vibrations. . . . I could actually distinguish the cornets, the roll of the drums, deep-toned violas and violins singing in exquisite unison. . . . As I listened, with darkness and melody, shadow and sound filling all the room, I could not help remembering that the great composer who poured forth such a flood of sweetness into the world was deaf like myself. I marveled at the power of his quenchless spirit by which out of his pain he wrought such joy for others—and there I sat, feeling with my hand the magnificent symphony which broke like a sea upon the silent shores of his soul and mine."[4]

Many big ideas are inaudible or invisible. Yet these intangibles are essential in supporting community life. To encourage opportunities for connecting with big ideas, libraries must create an appropriate everyday ambience through those we hire, the programs and services we offer, and the collections we develop. Libraries need workers who have compassion and the ability to spark curiosity in themselves and others. Library programs and services should inspire people to think, create, and contribute to society. Access to great books and information offers the opportunity for everyone in a community to explore ideas, pursue being their best, and give voice to their contributions.

The eighteenth-century German playwright and poet Friedrich Schiller described joy as the means to creativity—a good place to start—and to higher-level thinking. In wedding the good with the beautiful and cultivating our sensitivity to both—by cultivating the best within us and the best within the world—we do not become slaves to the dark side of nature and do not squander "our citizenship in the intelligible world." How can we avoid becoming slaves to negativity, especially in the midst of a challenge? How can we wed the best skills and splendor of our fellow human beings in our collaborative efforts despite facing difficulties?

The library can be an uplifting spirit in a community and a great source of inspiration. We don't have to be the U.S. president, a bestselling author, a world-renowned playwright, or a famous poet to tap into and activate big ideas.

How can you recognize a big idea from a small or stupid one? A big idea will offer insights to help solve a problem. It will provide a stimulus in the mind to act and create. If an idea is a big one, work with it and expand its use in your daily activity. A small idea will have limitations, but it can still be useful to understand and express a big idea.

As we cross the bridge of enlightenment to tap big ideas, we discover that big ideas and helpful small ideas can be connected. The big ideas of joy and optimism can lead to a storehouse of daily cheerfulness. The big idea of helpfulness can bolster our ability to be kind and considerate to everyone in any circumstances. The big idea of unity can help the growth of forgiveness and patience in our ever-expanding maturity. The key is to think through and explore the meaning and purpose of the big idea, determine its value, and activate it in our daily life.

Unimportant small ideas and stupid ideas—which do not support the effort to enlighten humanity—should be changed or dropped. For example, a library program that discusses only the anger and hurt expressed in an author's memoir misses an opportunity to promote the big ideas of respect, goodwill, and unity.

Plato came up with the word *idea* (in modern philosophy, this has been translated as the English word *form*). Although the word *idea* has been dumbed down to mean "something understood," the original significance of the word referred to the "look of a thing," an archetype, and "to see," the act of thinking.

Hindu philosophy examines how we can interact with the mental essence that underlies the truth of a situation. Ralph Waldo Emerson said of Hindu writings, "I have found eternal compensation, unfathomable power, and unbroken peace [in them]." Emerson along with Nathaniel Hawthorne, Wilhelm von Humboldt, and Mark Twain were among many writers, educators, and philosophers of the West who studied and valued Hindu philosophical traditions for successful living.

For example, the human expression of goodwill can be expanded by understanding the perception of the life-force on three levels of energy—the general, the subtle, and the abstract. "To update the Hindu idea, we can say that energy is said to consist of three levels—the level of appearance, the level of inner meaning, and the level of abstract essence. The mind learns to separate ideas into these levels. For example, the three levels of a chair are the physical level, the design of the chair, and the abstract principle of *sitting*," says Carl Japikse, author of *What's the Big Idea?* As we create our collaborative learning spaces, innovation labs, and "literacy playgrounds" in our library buildings, we can ponder the purpose of curiosity in the library. We can further connect to the essence of play, the value of thinking, and the love of learning to guide the design of library spaces.

Goodwill is the life-force that unites humanity. The ideas or concepts that help us express goodwill include respect for the best within others, compassion to awaken our willingness to help make things better, and reverence to cherish, love, and enjoy life.

Plato's *Symposium* asserts that inspired human thinking has its origin in universal big ideas. Young people should visit beautiful ideas, says Plato, and be guided by the ideal of creating "fair thoughts."

Plato makes the case that when "youth" tune into and explore big ideas, they learn that the beauty of a big idea is "akin to the beauty of another" big idea. If the beauty or benefit within a big idea is a person's pursuit, "how foolish" would they be not to recognize that the beauty in every big idea "is one and the same"! In other words, big ideas may serve different functions—integrity, joy, or ingenuity—but each contributes to the same "good" results of enlightening humanity. They can be traced back to an original or universal design to benefit humanity, while silly and stupid ideas do not have their roots in any beneficial purpose.

An incomplete list of big ideas includes the essence of the following:

• Harmony	• Dignity	• Synthesis
• Opportunity	• Unity	• Renewal
• Joy	• Truth	• Goodwill
• Maturity	• Growth	• Wisdom
• Grace	• Intuition	• Optimism
• Gratitude	• Adaptability	• Cooperation
• Freedom	• Objectivity	• Humility
• Nobility	• Creativity	• Reverence

- Exuberance
- Peace
- Excellence
- Curiosity

- Duty
- Tolerance
- Contentment
- Helpfulness

- Respect
- Ingenuity
- Integrity
- Beauty

Examples of *small but valid ideas* that can help put big ideas into action include the following:

- Kindness
- Patience
- Forgiveness
- Sharing
- Consideration
- Zest
- Persistence
- Empathy
- Determination
- Bravery

- Industriousness
- Self-Sufficiency
- Humor
- Motivation
- Conscientiousness
- Self-Control
- Self-Reliance
- Common Sense
- Concentration
- Discernment

- Logic
- Contemplation
- Analysis
- Cheerfulness
- Generosity
- Enthusiasm
- Responsibility
- Self-Discipline
- Aspiration
- Resilience

These ideas are truly a treasure housed by each library. Whether we tap into them or not, the opportunity is there for all librarians to celebrate these ideas.

It is not the purpose of this book to examine all these ideas. Individual library staffers can explore them. However, it is useful to know about big ideas that oversee, govern, and influence how to bring out the best in ourselves, others, and society. When we harness gratitude, for example, and focus it on the talents, strengths, and achievements of ourselves and others, we are better able to make sense of circumstances, solve problems, and see that most people are basically decent and caring.

An etymology dictionary can help us trace ideas back to their original meaning and function. This understanding gives us insights into what is a small versus a stupid idea. Small idea examples that are *unimportant* and *unhelpful* and may actually be stupid, foolish, or even harmful when implemented include blame, envy, worry, self-pity, doubt, and confusion.

Blame promotes a doom-and-gloom outlook. The history of the word *blame* can be traced back to Old French "to condemn, criticize" and Latin "to revile, reproach." The idea of blaming others or our life circumstances acts as a distraction from moving things forward and keeps us mired in a cesspool of unhelpful—and often harmful—ideas.

Through reading, pondering, and promoting great thinkers, such as Ralph Waldo Emerson, Nathaniel Hawthorne, William Shakespeare, Edgar Allan Poe, Helen Keller, Abraham Lincoln, and Charles Dickens, librarians provide a jumping-off place to big ideas. Aristotle wrote in the *Nicomachean Ethics* "for the things we have to learn before we can do them, we learn by doing them."

Whether through "hands-on" activities, discussion programs, technology training, or access to information resources, a library can enhance an individual's efforts to cross the bridge to enlightenment. Libraries offer opportunities for people to learn skills, think for themselves, and fulfill their potential. Libraries help people turn to and explore uplifting big ideas and minimize their consideration of stupid or silly ideas.

If we are uncertain about resolving a problem, we can work with the big ideas of curiosity and optimism to use the information we already have to explore and try new steps. If we are struggling with difficult people, we can use tolerance and harmony to get along with them. If we are discouraged, we can explore the big ideas of gratitude and renewal to gain confidence and cheerfulness to deal with challenging situations.

FIGURE 6.1

An example of the big idea of cooperation is a community's effort to create a large (14,000 sq. ft.) library makerspace project. Carroll County (MD) Public Library will open Exploration Commons at 50 East in 2020. Exploration Commons will feature a technology-focused makerspace, a professional teaching kitchen, and meeting and collaboration spaces.

Rendering courtesy of Manns Woodward Studios

When a public library, local career and tech high school, community college, and technology businesses collaborate to promote lifelong learning opportunities through a new library makerspace, they can tap and apply the big idea of cooperation. They can demonstrate the value that is added to their programs and services when they plan and work together. Cooperation gives these organizations the ability to listen and respond together in order to serve the community at large. "We are delighted to support the library's Exploration Commons at 50 East to expand and influence technology resources in the community. Libraries are an integral part of our education and technology ecosystem and a place where every citizen is able to access cutting-edge technology and resources at a minimal cost. It'll help us connect people interested in developing their technology skills to a network of over 520 county employers—and vice versa. In this way, the library makerspace is helping the community put skills into action," says Kati Townsley, executive director of the Carroll Technology Council. Cooperation at this level turns a good makerspace into a top-notch destination for activating and advancing individual potential.

James and Deborah Fallows's book *Our Towns: A 100,000-Mile Journey into the Heart of America* describes libraries as offering "a genuine look into the heart and soul" of a community. It is important that libraries do the heavy lifting of connecting people with ideas. Today's library staffers in all types of libraries—whether serving a student body, a client group, or the general public in a small town—have a golden opportunity and, indeed, a steadfast responsibility to lead the way in exploring and activating big ideas.

NOTES

1. Wayne Bivens-Tatum, *Libraries and the Enlightenment* (Los Angeles: Library Juice, 2012), 1.
2. Madeleine L'Engle, from a lecture at the Library of Congress, November 16, 1983, to celebrate children's books.
3. Helen Keller, *Optimism* (1903; Marble Hill, GA: Entheas, 2006), 27–28.
4. *The Auricle* 2, no. 6 (March 1924), American Foundation for the Blind, Helen Keller Archives.

PART III

Implementing Ideas

7

The Lark Ascending

Thinking is the hardest work there is, which
is probably the reason why so few engage in it.

—HENRY FORD

What's the value of a big idea, such as grace, unless we express it? If we only talk about the value of harmony but do nothing with it, how does this improve life? If we discover a fresh sense of humor and a dollop of wisdom in a Sandra Boynton picture book, do we share it with every child—and adult—we know? When we are uplifted by composer Ralph Vaughn Williams's *The Lark Ascending*, do we listen again and again to explore its beauty and try to integrate it into all that we think, say, and do? Do we read and ponder the insights of Plato, Hippocrates, Benjamin Franklin, and Paramahansa Yogananda and activate them in our work and domestic lives? Can we make the effort to read or attend a performance of *The Merchant of Venice* and learn about mercy?

Who else in a school or a town, or a medical center or a college has the expertise, resources, and opportunity to learn to think, but the librarian? Who else has the ability to offer that skill to others? Who else can cross the bridge to enlightenment of big ideas and show others how to do so *without badgering*? Who else can nurture an individual—no matter what the person's age, background, or level of intellect—to explore a big idea and reflect slowly and carefully about that idea *without nagging* the person? Who else can champion big ideas and help others learn to express and integrate them—*by extending an open invitation without pressuring, lecturing, or pestering*? Librarians, of course! We are learning to value the ability to think things through, to treasure common sense, and thus reinforce the overarching purpose of a library: to enlighten humanity.

The role of the library is to be helpful and bring forth big ideas through its collections, activities, and services. Interacting with big ideas requires our ability to ponder. A big idea—like the art of reading—has three levels of comprehension—superficial, meaning, and power. When we read a romance or mystery novel, this may be considered superficial but enjoyable reading for light entertainment. When we "speed-read" a business article or library policy to garner essential facts, we may gain a good understanding of the content, but it's still at a superficial level because we are not spending time to ponder the content.

Using the phrase "as brave as a lion" is a superficial way to describe the big idea of *courage*. However, we can use those few words as a portal to a more thoughtful, mental, or inner understanding of the nature and expression of courage. Plato promoted courage as one of the four principles for mature living in *The Republic*. In the dialogue called *Laches*, Socrates and others discuss the meaning of courage as strength of heart. Nicias, a character in the dialogue, says: "There is a difference, to my way of thinking, between fearlessness and courage . . . thoughtful courage is a quality possessed by very few, but that rashness and boldness, and fearlessness, which has no forethought, are very common qualities possessed by many men, many women, many children, many animals."

It takes thoughtful courage to

- make decisions about programs, policies, funding, and a myriad of library details;
- minimize the time spent on nonessential activities—the author Stephen Covey described such activities as "not important and not urgent"—in order to concentrate on top priorities;
- make adjustments to serve our community's hour of need and—at the same time—help fulfill the long-term service of humanity; and
- set aside tiredness, stress, and other distractions in order to stay focused on the work at hand.

The purpose of courage is to support us as we act on our convictions. Courage is a key ingredient for being helpful. Understanding courage takes thinking. The thinking process includes the ability to select excellent resources, read carefully, and *ponder and think through the idea completely and thoroughly*.

Cooperation is a big idea reflected in sayings such as "Many hands make light work," "All for one, and one for all," and "All hands on deck." By researching and pondering the word *cooperation*, we find that it translates to "working together" and "to have effect, be active"—stemming from the Latin. These phrases are tied to "synergy," derived from the Greek *synergia* or "assistance, help; joint work, cooperation."

The sayings, phrases, and words related to "cooperation" give us a starting point to dispel the erroneous notion that cooperation means people can dictate exactly what others should be doing. This kind of "cooperation" becomes pressure on the work group. Declaring it cooperation doesn't make it so. As we strive to help others, we cannot assume that our colleagues have mastered the right cooperation.

It is hoped that sayings, clichés, and other quick ways that help us recognize and become aware of big ideas at a cursory level will stimulate thinking. They can serve as a jumping-off point to help us go beyond the words to a deeper understanding of a big idea.

In order to interact with big ideas, we need to read slowly so that we are reading *to think*. For example, when reading to ponder and think through the ideas of Benjamin Franklin, Mark Twain, and Saki, we may read thirty pages an hour—as opposed to fifty pages an hour for a light novel or mystery. When reading and pondering William Shakespeare, Ralph Waldo Emerson, and Plato, the reading-to-think pace might be only ten or fifteen pages an hour.

No matter what great writer or thinker we are reading, the goal is to get us to think. Thinking is the mechanism to go beyond the superficial level. Librarians can encourage and nudge people to commune with big ideas in order to tap the meaning and power of each idea.

The role of the librarian is to challenge, nurture, and draw forth the best within ourselves and the people we serve. Helping to train people to develop the skills of reading-to-think, pondering to gain insights, exploring to discover, and thinking completely and thoroughly is central to what libraries can and should offer. The way to fulfill this role is to strive for the ability to be patient yet encouraging, gentle yet courageous, and curious yet discerning.

A superficial level of understanding *truth* may be seen in Alexander Pope's phrase, "Tis but a part we see, and not a whole." If we read Pope's "Essay on Man," his philosophical poem from the 1730s, we can discover more about "truth" or the whole of life—*if* we slowly ponder, explore, and then express it. If we work, for example, in a unit or department of a library, we don't automatically have a far-reaching perspective or full understanding of the organization's functioning and effectiveness. We need to ponder, explore, and discover broader insights. We need to think like the director or CEO. Similarly, if we operate with a limited viewpoint about life and never ask the right questions—questions that lead us to improving life—we are likely to know only one spoke of the wheel. As we expand our knowledge and understanding, there is no limit to tapping the meaning and power behind each big idea.

PRAISEWORTHY AND BEAUTIFUL

While individuals, organizations, or groups may try to pressure others into conforming to their way of thinking, the librarian is poised and ready to help people think thoroughly and completely in order to make their own decisions. Librarians can help trace ideas back to their origin to determine whether the ideas are big, small, or silly or harmful. For example, Aristotle taught the "golden mean" in his *Nicomachean Ethics* as the ideal harmony between two extremes, one of excess and the other of deficiency. The idea of the golden mean can be traced as well to Confucius, Buddha, and other great thinkers. No matter what the historical or cultural reference, this big idea is universal and timeless. Librarians can explore the golden mean for themselves and guide people to resources to discover the concept on their own. Finding and choosing the golden mean may not be quick and easy, but it is worthwhile and should be celebrated. As Aristotle said, work that aims at the ideal of harmony is work well done and is "praiseworthy and beautiful."[1]

Some people try to dictate what others should think, say, and do—promoting a groupthink mentality. They may be unable to tolerate a different viewpoint and will attempt to force their way of thinking on others, either gently or grimly. They may nudge or badger librarians to conform to their groupthink framework. Either way, the goal is clearly to pressure the library to take on an advocacy role for their own personal cause.

Some individuals whose goal is the same—to pressure the library to advocate for them—are less direct. They may promote a "don't berate, instead relate" approach and make an effort to tolerate a different viewpoint, although this is usually temporary. They may give lip service to being open to learning something new as long as it doesn't shatter their underlying groupthink structure. However, "don't berate, instead relate" has a similar goal: to push librarians to advocate for a personal cause or fad instead of fulfilling the library's purpose to enlighten humanity.

How can we help people discover big ideas, and ponder and explore them beyond the superficial level—in order to understand and express these ideas effectively? It can be helpful for librarians to be aware of effective practices. However, it's also important to discern that the practices of others may not work in every situation, nor will they necessarily have staying power. Learning to think creatively or to think thoroughly and completely can add value to our operations, services, and programs—no matter what our current level of excellence is.

Plato described thinking as "the talking of the soul with itself." Plato was the student of Socrates and the teacher of Aristotle. These three ancient Greek philosophers reached a superior level of practical, inspirational, and wise thinking. Although humanity and civilization have advanced since ancient Greece in many and magnificent ways, we should continue to learn from

Socrates, Plato, and Aristotle in developing our thinking skills. The ability to think with a sense of exploration and discovery helps anyone of any age, background, or income level tune into big ideas.

CALMING REASSURANCE

The phrase "above the fray" has been used in recent years by a company that designs ways to organize technology to make life less complicated. A consulting group uses the same phrase to describe how parents can help their children safely maneuver digital and online activity. However, we don't want to fixate on "the fray," but rather focus our attention on conveying the power of big ideas, such as optimism, respect, and mercy. We want to *stay above* the fray and cultivate our clarity of thinking. Then we can better reflect and commune with these universal ideas—which have been around for a long time and will continue to be around with the help of librarians.

The ability to laugh—gently and kindly—gives us an advantage in staying above the fray in order to think clearly. Humor delivered with a gracious and open heart is a golden asset—as opposed to thoughtless and uncaring "funny" observations about the oddities of life. Laughter helps us interact with life without being stamped into the ground. This strength leads to the ability to think at higher levels and maintain a sense of curiosity under any circumstances. Laughing gently *with* ourselves and others, not "at them," can help us minimize taking life too seriously and boost our ability to think. It offers a tool to help us focus on the calming reassurance of staying above the fray.

But it was Socrates, Benjamin Franklin, and other great thinkers who set a high standard for using calming reassurance to get above and *stay above* the fray during life's difficult struggles, disagreements with colleagues, and assaults by harsh critics.

In Plato's *Apology*, Socrates is characterized as striving to expose the arrogance and deception of the "wisdom" of Athens's elders. His enemies falsely accused Socrates of corrupting the city's youth—by asking questions and encouraging them to think thoroughly, creatively, and completely. Libraries have something in common with this effort—they provide people with resources, activities, and services in order to encourage them to think for themselves.

The Athenian leaders charged and condemned Socrates to death, but this turned out to be an unpopular decision because he was understood and cherished by the Athenian people. One night the door to his jail cell was unlocked by an adversary with the hope that Socrates would "escape" and thus save the face of the corrupt rulers. Socrates stayed in jail. He was executed "by the drinking of hemlock" as scheduled the following day. Socrates stayed above the fray, and ultimately sacrificed himself for the greater good. Librarians of today do not experience this level of condemnation or sacrifice in their efforts to help enlighten humanity. However, Socrates is a model for librarians to demonstrate the value of helping people to think for themselves and think things through.

Another inspiring example is Benjamin Franklin, a writer, inventor, scientist, and polymath who has been called the "first citizen of eighteenth-century America." He was personally attacked during a political hearing before a London council in 1774 over what became known as the Hutchinson Letters Affair. But at the hearing Franklin comported himself with dignity and restraint in the face of unexpected, unwarranted, and pernicious attacks on his character.

At the hearing England's solicitor-general, Alexander Wedderburn, harangued Franklin for an hour. "I had the grievous mortification to hear Mr. Wedderburn," reported William Bollan, a lawyer and colleague of Franklin, "wandring from the proper question before their Lordships, pour forth such a torrent of virulent abuse on Dr. Franklin as never before took place within the compass of my knowledge of judicial proceedings, his reproaches appearing to me incompatible with the principles of law, truth, justice, propriety, and humanity."[2]

Franklin rose above *and* stayed above the fray by maintaining a calm and positive demeanor while conveying "philosophic tranquility." When finally asked to answer the charges, he did not overreact, but instead responded by remaining silent, turning, and exiting the room with dignity. Franklin told friends afterwards that he was in "good conscience" about his decisions in the affair over which he had been insulted. (Moreover, the humiliation that Franklin had endured at the hearing convinced him that his efforts to conciliate relations between Great Britain and the American colonies were hopeless, and thereafter he became one of the foremost proponents of the struggle for American independence.)

Librarians can turn to Socrates in 399 BC and Franklin in 1774 as heroic examples of how to think things through and serenely stay above the fray of hurly-burly, brouhaha, gobbledygook, and even death. The phrase "staying above the fray" is a concept for librarians to ponder, embrace, and activate.

Can library staffers maintain skilled detachment, practice a neutral attitude, and seek the golden mean on the job when it comes to opposing views on a topic? Yes! Should librarians cultivate objectivity, goodwill, and discernment when approached about a sensitive issue? Yes, absolutely!

Values are sculpted by the mind and establish a foundation for inner strength—no matter if we are feeling annoyed or tolerant. If a library considers "love of learning" a core value, each employee should embrace the idea of learning new things. Library staff value wisdom and the application of knowledge. It doesn't matter whether someone working in a library happens to be

FIGURE 7.1

Benjamin Franklin staying above the fray during his unwarranted and mean-spirited public humiliation before the Privy Council. Nineteenth-century engraving by Robert Whitechurch (1814–1880).

SOURCE: Library of Congress https://www.loc.gov/exhibits/treasures/franklin-break .html)— U.S. National Archives and Records Administration, Public Domain

in a good or bad mood on a particular day; the love of learning motivates each person to fulfill the library's underlying purpose to help enlighten humanity through books, information, programs, and services.

The founding of the American republic was based on deep-seated values like the love of learning, religious freedom, and the entrepreneurial spirit. Thousands of people sold their belongings, paid passage, and risked their lives to sail to Pennsylvania, Maryland, New England, and other colonies to make a fresh start. The risk was high. The learning curve to stay above the fray in order to survive was steep. Intelligent risk-taking and learning to think things through connect us with the big ideas of optimism, dignity, humility, and gratitude that have helped communities succeed and flourish.

Librarians nurture practical skills to discover ideas and engage with abstract thought so that we can apply our values in what we think, say, and do. When facing a challenge, correcting a mistake, or handling embarrassment, do we stay above the fray or hubbub in order to be helpful? "I appreciate that libraries have reliable tools—such as objectivity, neutrality, and discernment—to apply in any given sensitive situation while effectively serving everyone in the community," says Jennifer Ranck, director of the Worcester County (MD) Library.

George Meredith's poem "The Lark Ascending" can help librarians learn to think with clarity, make helpful decisions, and be, as Franklin described, in "good conscience."

> He rises and begins to round,
> He drops the silver chain of sound,
> Of many links without a break,
> In chirrup, whistle, slur and shake . . .
>
> For singing till his heaven fills,
> 'Tis love of earth that he instils,
> And ever winging up and up,
> Our valley is his golden cup,
> And he the wine which overflows
> To lift us with him as he goes . . .

The English composer Ralph Vaughn Williams was inspired by this poem to create his stunning instrumental work of the same name. How can librarians help the "golden cup" of ideas overflow and awaken the good, the beautiful, and the best in each other and in those we serve?

Hilary Hahn, a Grammy award–winning violinist who delivers a refreshing interpretation of *The Lark Ascending,* has perfected the ability to perform without pretense. She honors the music and presents herself without any affectation. Describing the benefit of playing a piece of music for an audience, Hahn says that "playing a piece on stage is at a whole different level. Things jump out at you that you never noticed before. I think when you're performing, you subconsciously pick up on what the audience is reacting to and that's why it changes."

A musician, like a librarian, can lead an individual or group to the big ideas of life. Inspired musicians can be so in touch with a big idea in rehearsal that they tailor their interpretation in anticipation of the audience's needs. They are above ordinary thought and focus on leading the audience to the big idea. The most effective musicians—and librarians—do not shove the big idea onto people, but strive to know and meet the needs of each person or audience member ahead of time when preparing and rehearsing. In this way, people will be challenged in the right way to ponder, absorb, and commune with the music and the big idea behind it.

Hahn demonstrates how to use curiosity: "I try having a finished interpretation at every concert, but if I just stick to that, I'm going to miss out. So it's really important to me to stay open to these things that come up in the moment, reveal themselves. That shows me where I really want to go."

Librarians can practice curiosity and tailor a big idea to each patron, student, and visitor. Like musicians, we know from serving people in the library that each person responds differently. We are at our best when we stay open to each person's potential. We can help people be their best by extending an open invitation to commune with big ideas without insisting, preaching, or nagging. We librarians can best connect our community or clientele to big ideas when we, like the lark ascending, lift up and stay above the "valley" by thinking with clarity and being open to unlimited possibilities.

NOTES

1. Aristotle, *Nicomachean Ethics,* ed. and trans. Joe Sachs (Newburyport, MA: Focus Publishing, R. Pullins, 2002), 32–35.
2. Massachusetts Historical Society Collection, ix (1897), 338, cited within National Archives website entry, "The Final Hearing before the Privy Council Committee for Plantation Affairs on the Petition from the Massachusetts House of Representatives for the Removal of Hutchinson and Oliver, 29 January 1774," https://founders.archives.gov/documents/Franklin/01-21-02-0018.

8

Ingenuity

Common sense is genius dressed in working clothes.

—RALPH WALDO EMERSON

Did you not know? Have you not heard?

Genius lies in each person. Inspired librarians can gently, skillfully, and joyously draw it forth in themselves and others. Elizabeth Barrett Browning described genius as "the power of expressing a new individuality." The word *genius* can be traced back to the Proto-Indo-European, Latin, and Old English languages relating to an "innate quality," "to seize" big ideas, and develop a "mental ability" to express them—from optimism to harmony to creativity.

The correct idea of creativity is required for seizing big ideas and drawing forth our best innate qualities. Creativity is a means for expanding the best of one's natural and acquired capacities—for learning about and developing our inner genius.

Creativity helps us tap into Aristotle's "golden mean." The golden mean, as Aristotle suggests, focuses on the middle ground between two extremes, steering between too much and too little. This point of excellence can help us explore, discover, and expand our understanding and ability to get things done.

We can use the golden mean as a platform to launch our thinking— our pondering—and help us figure out complex problems, make effective decisions, and use big ideas to help our library service shine. For example, we can ponder "cowardice" as defined as too little confidence and compare it to "rashness" as too much confidence in order to discover the golden mean between them in "confidence." We can reflect on "cowardice" as defined as too much fear, and then "foolhardiness" as too little fear. We can use genius to find "courage" in creativity, which requires a bit of the fool to go beyond conventional thinking. We librarians can convey this process of thinking to the people we help. This work—aiming at the golden mean and exploring beyond the mean—takes time, practice, and patience, but it can expand our scope of thinking, our capacity for understanding, and our potential for serving others through libraries. As Aristotle suggests, it may not be easy to do, but the effort is joyful, dignified, and commendable.

CREATIVE THINKING

Have you ever heard of Dr. Edward de Bono? Probably not. If not, you are missing something here. If you have heard of him, do you include him in your thinking about learning to be creative in new and effective ways? De Bono—an author, Maltese physician, and philosopher with past faculty appointments at the universities of Oxford, London, Cambridge, and Harvard—invented a concept called *lateral thinking* in the late 1960s and developed an exercise called the Six Thinking Hats. Lateral thinking, the Six Thinking Hats, and other de Bono "tools" can be used for group discussion or individual reflection. De Bono is considered by many around the world to be a leading authority on creative thinking. He helps us use the mind in a practical and intentional manner to gain insights. With some practice, his thinking activities can be helpful every time they are used.

The Six Thinking Hats evoke different aspects of our thinking abilities—objectivity (white hat), best possible outcome (yellow), intuition (red),

FIGURE 8.1

More than 100,000 people have been trained in the Six Thinking Hats in 35 countries. For more information, see de Bono's *Six Thinking Hats* (1985) and his other books or go to www.edwdebono.com and www.debonogroup.com/six_think ing_hats.php.

SOURCE: Mindwerx International

potential downside (black), new perspectives (green), and summary and next steps (blue). For example, in a thirty-minute group discussion using the Six Hats method, members of a public library's outreach department created a fresh attitude and new perspective on serving people beyond library walls. Over the next year, their efforts produced a 50 percent increase from 10,000 to 15,000 people reached through outreach activities.

Six Thinking Hats Activity

1. Think of an issue or a problem you might want to solve. Or think of an idea or a plan you'd like to implement. Express it in one sentence. For example: How can the library serve people in alternative ways to uplift, inspire, and enrich their lives?

2. Choose a "hat" to begin. Often, this is blue, for how I should think about it. For example, what feelings need to be considered? What about future consequences? What do we need to learn first?

3. Go through all six hats and keep notes on your observations
    1. White—what facts do I need and how do I get them?
    2. Red—how do I feel about all of this?
    3. Black—what is the potential downside? How can I prevent it?
    4. Yellow—what are all the possible advantages/benefits? What is the best possible outcome?
    5. Green—what new approaches can I generate? How can I see this problem in a new way?
    6. Blue—review and sum up what I have learned in this process. Next step?

Adapted from *Six Thinking Hats* by Edward de Bono

We library staffers can be most effective if we apply integrity and excellence in ways that go beyond ourselves and our organization—in order to think creatively for those we serve. Creativity is related not only to traditional inspiration in terms of creating music and art, but can also be developed by each of us to enrich our thinking in all areas of life. We can teach ourselves to be creative when we

- write grant proposals that sparkle,
- plan a staff training on customer service that inspires,
- select a new software that strengthens office collaboration, and
- stay above the fray during a battle of opposing viewpoints (not that we'd take one side or the other) in order to harness

equilibrium during a book discussion—all for the good of the library.

The word *creativity* gets a lot of lip service today, but unfortunately, it seldom goes much further. Positive thinking can be a good starting point for learning to think completely and thoroughly—but to embrace creativity, thinking must become more profound. Some definitions emphasize that creativity is primarily a function of the brain or intellectual capacity, but this is mistaken. Other misguided interpretations give us creative permission to be clumsy, chaotic, crummy, lazy, or boring. *Creativity is a disciplined mental state of realization.* It is not driven by emotional euphoria or anger. We become aware of big ideas, plant seeds to cultivate those ideas, and bring them to fruition.

Creativity is a dynamic process of tapping inspiration, nourishing the mind with big ideas, and bringing forth something into society and culture which is new and will benefit humanity. But tapping inspiration alone is not enough. Creativity goes further. It fills us with awe, but not emotional fluff. Creativity is accessible, but not without a structure of self-control and poise. It is not an excuse to feel overly relaxed and never get anything done. *Creativity requires an intense curiosity about life and all the wonder of life. It helps us reveal the presence and potential of the best within people and circumstances.* How can we develop a new training to teach librarians how to conduct online instruction? How should we approach a fundraising campaign to magnetically draw those—who are interested—into supporting the library?

The significance of creativity is that it brings something new, implicit, praiseworthy, and pleasing into the world. It takes a little know-how, awareness, and effort, but it is accessible to all. Creativity is an open invitation for everyone, no matter their background, education, and connections or lack thereof. It is an innate process for each of us to promote the art of living—bringing out the best in ourselves and others. It is a lifelong, worthwhile, and joyful goal. The built-in human impulse to grow, learn, and add something compelling to life can help us seek ongoing relationships, opportunities, and experiences to do so.

Creativity enables people to contribute to life in order to benefit humanity, whether through important and expansive actions or in modest and seemingly insignificant ways. No matter what the type of contribution—improving a recipe by combining ingredients in new ways to delight family and friends, inventing a new sustainable solvent recovery system, designing a new collaborative library space, or expressing a new level of patience and kindness to a coworker—creativity is at our fingertips to help.

Creativity is an awe-inspiring, universal force that can be harnessed to enlighten humanity. Each of us can participate because our mind is part of the unlimited wisdom of life. Whatever we do, whoever we are, life is designed—if we pay attention—for everyone to touch the wellsprings of inspiration, joy, curiosity, and strength, and to use these big ideas to make a contribution to our work, domestic life, community, and civilization.

Like Abraham Lincoln, we can practice caring leadership in our library collaborations and promote charity for all viewpoints; like Shakespeare, we can provoke greater understanding of life and an appreciation of dignity and courage through great drama and poetry; like Nikola Tesla, we can explore the potential of genius and train the mind to think in ways to rise above the level of the obvious by emulating his style of working and thinking; like Mark Twain, we can rejuvenate ourselves through inspired fiction and humor and help others to do the same who may be tired, overly serious, or gloomy; like Helen Keller, we can use optimism, resilience, and joy to see obstacles as opportunities; like Richard Wagner, we can explore and strive to bring about the qualities of beauty, heroism, triumph, and glory through musical resources and events; and like Buddha, we can express the ideal of compassion by helping people fulfill their potential through library services and activities.

HARNESSING THE POWER OF CREATIVITY

Plato gives us a framework for learning about the interplay between discovering and examining big ideas and bringing insights and understanding into our work and domestic lives. He helps us develop creative thinking in terms of what works and what doesn't work when thinking completely and thoroughly. Anyone can train themselves to use a big idea as a starting point for creative thinking—for blending human and universal thinking. Human thinking includes the abstract—dealing with big ideas—and the concrete—applying them. Through reading, pondering, and contemplation, we can intuitively look for a hint or two to help us "connect the dots" in order to harness the power of genuine thinking and put it to work. For example, in his dialogue called *Parmenides,* Plato gives a hint about the big idea of unity when he explains, "That which is one is both a whole and has a part . . . each of the parts is not a part of many, but of a whole."[1]

Aristotle, a student of Plato and the teacher of Alexander the Great, helped to codify thinking by teaching us to ask the right questions in order to draw the right conclusions. Most of us learn this type of traditional or analytical thinking in school—it is sometimes referred to as "vertical" thinking. This type is finite and sequential in identifying an answer. Finding a solution is based on moving forward one step at a time. We rule out what doesn't work in the quest to find what does work—and hope to arrive at a beneficial answer. This kind of vertical thinking is useful, pragmatic, and needed for success.

However, to be thorough in our thinking we need to enrich Aristotle's analytical or vertical thinking—by doing more than asking questions and drawing conclusions—with what de Bono calls lateral thinking. "Rightness is what matters in vertical thinking. Richness is what matters in lateral thinking. Vertical thinking selects a pathway by excluding other pathways. Lateral thinking does not select but seeks to open up other pathways," explains de Bono.

We can use both vertical and lateral thinking to assess the needs and interests of people who are using the library and those who are not. Vertical thinking is a step-by-step path, starting with a question such as: *What more can the library do for you?* Requests to increase one-on-one assistance, provide collaborative learning spaces, or expand cultural arts programming provide direct feedback that can help us narrow down the ways to modify and improve services.

Lateral thinking is not a step-by-step method—A to B to C to D—but one that may jump from A to S via E—with S offering a far better solution than D. We can use diverse aspects of our thinking abilities such as speculating on the best scenario, planting and nurturing new seeds of growth, tapping and exploring observation, neutrality, objectivity, intuition, hunches, carefulness, caution, optimism, benefits, focus, control, summary, and reaching conclusions. We can discover new directions, potential, and genius within ourselves and others.

Together vertical and lateral thinking produce a more effective or thorough method of thinking through our ideas. Combining the two approaches leads to reflecting, pondering, or meditating on a challenge or project in ways that involve different facets of our thinking abilities. This expanded thinking method builds on our talent to use different thinking skills to reach a new level of productive work and creativity.

Vertical or analytical thinking is taught in school and is commonly used in life. Lateral thinking, on the other hand, requires practice and is a deliberate process to help us develop the skills related to creativity, insight, and humor. For example, lateral thinking can be effective as a ten-minute self-reflection activity that can help us move from a good idea—for example, conducting a library research project—to a great idea of harnessing the power of collaboration and goodwill within and outside the library organization.

A third alternative leading to creative thinking is the use of metaphors—familiar events or images that trigger a set of associations and possibilities when we dwell on them. These can convey useful ideas when we are searching for insights into solving problems or resolving challenges. Try this activity:

First—select a challenge or issue you would like to understand better.

Second—select a metaphor randomly from a list, such as the one below.

Third—think about how your challenge or issue is like the metaphor you have selected.

Fourth—use your imagination to ponder the associations of how the challenge and metaphor are similar.

- How can we overcome space limitations to create a makerspace area?
- Several of my staff and colleagues are hesitant about learning new and emerging technology. What should I do?

Here is a list of metaphors:

This project is like . . .

writing a novel.

having to clean out a cluttered closet.

being told you will soon need a new car.

learning to play a piano.

baking a big holiday meal.

planting a garden.

riding a bike on a windy day up a hill.

(Adapted from a creativity workshop taught by Robert Leichtman, M.D.)

A fourth alternative leading to creative thinking builds on both vertical and lateral thinking and is offered in Edgar Allan Poe's prose poem *Eureka*. Poe's genius can be seen not only in his invention of the detective story but also in his intuitive understanding, presented as a lecture and published as the essay *Eureka*, of the development and workings of the universe.

Using the scientific knowledge of the time, for example, Poe goes beyond the know-how of the 1840s to describe what would become understood as the Big Bang Theory and the mysteries of black holes and curved space a century or more later. He explains the motion of our solar system of planets around a sun and the motion of the Milky Way and other galaxies as concentric circles. However, he goes a step further by offering insights into the part that human beings play in the evolution of the universe. *Eureka* gives us a model for creative thinking—methodical, consistent, and uncomplicated.

FIGURE 8.2

American author, poet, and genius Edgar Allan Poe.

Photo image: Courtesy of Getty's Open Content Program

Poe's concept of using concentric circles as a visual and intuitive pathway to creativity gives us a practical method for expanding our thinking. Starting at the hub for inspiration and expanding outward, passing through each region between circles to the rim and back again, says Poe, offers a creative dance of inspired thinking. At the rim, we apply a big idea and examine what works and what doesn't work. We then take the idea back to the hub in order to ponder and draw on more inspiration. Poe invites the reader to learn the art of thinking beyond what is usually taught in school or college. He offers a solution-oriented process in which intuition plays a role in exploring big ideas and patterns. Albert Einstein called *Eureka* "a beautiful achievement of an unusually independent mind."

Human beings are designed to embody the big idea of dignity, for example. How can we apply this attribute at our customer service desk? By pondering dignity—at the hub—and exploring how it can be applied, we get a hint of its power. By expanding outward—to the rim—we harness the ability of dignity to bring out our best and make a difference in how we interact with others at the desk.

Dignity and other big ideas can impel us to great achievement in a seemingly mundane interaction at the service desk by bringing out the best of a customer's potential. We strive for excellence in cooperating and supporting our colleagues through the use of our talents and maturity. By using our own measure of dignity, we can set a good example for stakeholders to promote and spread dignity through collaboration. We can do the same with peace, optimism, respect, compassion, goodwill, and joy.

Another way to consider Poe's concept is by pondering how to tap and draw on the inspiration of a big idea at the hub of a thinking wheel, and then explore the idea's potential by taking it out to the rim—"where the rubber meets the road"—to apply and express the idea. Once we've learned about what works and what doesn't, we take the idea back to the hub in order to ponder it and draw on more inspiration. As we continue to take the idea back and forth—to the hub for inspiration, to the rim for application and expression—we learn how to further develop the idea's potential and translate it into new wisdom and innovation.

Libraries that have added value to a community, school, or university hark back to the roots of inspired thinking. However, if we take sides during a battle of opposing views, for example, we set up libraries to lose not only core customers, but casual customers as well. The more libraries can harness the power of neutrality, the more we can stay above the fray of divisiveness, be effective in enlightening humanity, and garner support from all sides. Taking sides creates unnecessary barriers.

"We encourage people to come to the library and try what we have to offer. Whether it's virtual reality free play, baby fun time, or reciting Shakespearean scripts with costumes and props, the library wants to encourage an intense curiosity about life to help each person recharge their enthusiasm for living," says Jillian Dittrich, manager of the Taneytown branch, Carroll County Public Library, Maryland. Talent is something that is acquired by studying and acquiring skills in a particular field over many years. Libraries are filled with resources to support any person's quest—including the librarian—to develop skills and learn to think creatively.

Reading and pondering excellent poetry is an example of a library resource to spur creative thinking. Talented English-speaking poets who have stood the test of time, such as Elizabeth Barrett Browning, Henry Wadsworth Long-fellow, and Alexander Pope, are at the ready on most library shelves. Poetry focuses thoughts into words that burst into seeds in the reader's mind to grow and expand our thinking. The power of poetry can help inspire, brighten, and boost our thinking beyond vertical thinking. Reading great poetry can open us to lateral thinking and above-the-mean comprehension.

The use of virtual reality interactives by NASA to experience live video of the Earth and Sun from the viewpoint of a satellite is another example of upcoming library offerings that can spur creative thinking. Alex Young, Ph.D., associate director for science at the Heliophysics Science Division of NASA Goddard, says, "We can observe the Sun's strong magnetic field and how it releases energy—a flash of light, we call a solar flare—into an electromagnetic spectrum that encompasses the Earth. This kind of exciting data is one example of how space weather science may inspire people of all ages to consider a career in space and flight."

We can strengthen our integrity in our work, learn to unlearn, and act—not react—to circumstances by using a blended approach where lateral thinking supplements vertical thinking. We can add Poe's concentric circles and his concept of getting inspired at the hub and expanding our thinking at the rim. Librarians can use these techniques to help ourselves and the people we serve to learn the art of thinking. We can help people draw forth and develop their genius.

NOTE

1. Plato, *The Dialogues of Plato Translated into English with Analyses and Introductions*, by B. Jowett, M.A. in Five Volumes, 3rd edition revised and corrected (Oxford University Press, 1892), https://oll.libertyfund.org/titles/768#Plato_0131-04_480.

9
Beauty through Goodwill and Helpfulness

Kindness is the language which the deaf
can hear and the blind can see.

—MARK TWAIN

In the mid-twentieth century, the Enoch Pratt Free Library in Baltimore and many other libraries across the country encouraged—and perhaps commanded—that we take particular care of our (paper) library card with the written phrase: "don't bend, fold, spindle, or mutilate." Imprinted on the card and in the awareness of millions of people was an implied message to cultivate the benefits of the library—and in turn, protect our inner greatness as members of humanity and rise above the mean to discover the enjoyment of lifelong learning.

> O beautiful library card,
>
> Your power unforeseen,
>
> Don't fold, spindle, or mutilate,
>
> Above the learned mean!

Seventy years later, librarians have the responsibility to see their role as a gateway to make sure we do not spindle the card of human growth. We have a long way to go to live up to this admonition. It's easy to bend, falsify, distort, or misinterpret the treasures of the library.

Learning about the big idea of beauty, for example, demonstrates that the common perspective that beauty falls only in the domain of artists, musicians, and poets is way too narrow. Although these creative types may be trailblazers for bringing beauty into daily life, beauty is not something that can be *created*; it is meant to be *revealed*. It is an intangible, important, and enduring element of every aspect of life—in nature, in the hearts, minds, and actions of humankind, and throughout the world and the universe. Beauty is to be unveiled by every person, not just artists and musicians—and that includes librarians.

As we study the great artists, composers, and writers, we learn that beauty is more than skin deep. We learn that it is not in the "eye of the beholder," but a quality that can be expressed and infused into life. The word *beauty*—a big idea—has historic roots related to "praise, revere, think well of," and "honor, make blessed, and celebrate." It is part of the excellence and quality of life—and originates above the "learned mean." From the tasks of creating a weekly staff schedule and preparing a team meeting agenda to delivering customer service with a sparkle in our eye and interacting with stakeholders in ways to harness the power of collaboration, beauty can be honored everywhere.

INSPIRATION VS. DULLNESS

The goal of tapping the big idea of beauty is not only to unveil it, but to transform that which is less than beautiful—and to do so even in the face of a barrage of something that is less than beautiful, such as anger, pessimism, worry, and fear—whether our own or that of a library customer. If we are short with a colleague or grumpy with a student, we poison the beauty we might otherwise express. The impulse to grow as an individual—and learn about beauty and other big ideas—helps librarians demonstrate this within ourselves while we help others grow as well.

The library is filled with treasures, masterpieces, and learned gems—but *without clear priorities*, it may be filled with dullness, mediocrity, and bunk. The library promotes the age of wisdom—but *without discernment*, it may promote an age of foolishness. The library is the gateway to Light and Inspiration—but *without tapping the overarching purpose to enlighten humanity*, it may become a gateway to Gloom and Doom. The library is a springboard to hope, joy, goodwill, and beauty—but *without big ideas*, it may get bogged down in pettiness and mislead humanity. The library is a portal to the enjoyment of lifelong learning—but *without sparking curiosity*, it may become a portal to aimless distraction. The library offers a cherished, safe space for all of us to grow in our thinking—but *without neutrality*, it may squelch the free exchange of ideas and encourage divisive poppycock.

Jonathan Swift's satire "The Battle of the Books," which was published in 1704 as an introduction to *A Tale of a Tub,* reflects the interplay of inspired thinking—and that which is not inspired—through a war of ideas between the "Ancients" and the "Moderns." In this satire, Homer oversees the horse soldiers for the Ancients; Plato and Aristotle command the bowmen; Hippocrates, the dragoons; and Vossius, a Dutch scholar and librarian, helps bring up the rear. The "battle" takes place in the King's Library at St. James Place in London.

Swift describes *war* as "the child of Pride, and Pride the daughter of Riches" and at the same time, nearly related to "Beggary and Want." The central concept of the war of ideas is between writers who enlighten humanity with inspiration, clarity, and wit and those who misguide and misinform humanity by spreading falsehoods, fakery, and tomfoolery.

Swift includes an allegory about inspiration versus dullness through an exchange between a bumblebee and a spider arguing high on a bookshelf in the midst of the battle. He infers that the spider—or anyone—trying to mislead others may build schemes "with as much method and skill as you please," but it will not have lasting power because it is built on fluff. "If the materials [of dull, small ideas] be nothing but dirt, spun out . . . into a cobweb; . . . [they] may be imputed to their being forgotten, or neglected, or hid in a corner."[1]

Whereas the bee—or anyone—making a good faith effort to be curious about the best in life and feed on the limitless nectar of inspired thinking will help spread beauty and goodwill. "I visit, indeed, all the flowers and blossoms of the field and garden, but whatever I collect thence enriches myself without the least injury to their beauty, their smell, or their taste. . . . We have rather chosen to till our hives with honey and wax; thus with the two noblest of things, which are sweetness and light."[2]

FIGURE 9.1

Woodcut of Swift's "The Battle of the Books," a satire representing the battle between big ideas and small ideas. The battle continues today but can be won with libraries playing a leading role.

Creative Commons Public Domain

This eighteenth-century battle did not end. A battle of thoughts is still raging today in the form of big ideas versus small ideas. One of the forces that guarantees winning is the big idea of goodwill.

GOODWILL

Goodwill can be described as the life-force that unites humanity. Respect, compassion, and reverence help us express goodwill. Respect helps us understand and appreciate others, compassion awakens our willingness to help make things better, and reverence cherishes, loves, and enjoys life. When we librarians learn to manage our own challenges and help ourselves by working with the big ideas of respect, compassion, and reverence, we are developing lifelong learning skills to express goodwill—which many customers need and humanity as a whole must learn. Librarians can play a role in uniting humanity by expressing goodwill. Shakespeare's Antonio, in *The Merchant of Venice*, compares the world to a stage where every person "must play a part." We can help ourselves and others learn to enjoy life and the role we each play—by interweaving respect, compassion, and reverence to express goodwill.

The big idea of *respect* does not imply approval, but it compels us to nurture growth in ourselves and others and helps us work with the wholeness of humanity—so that even when others act foolishly or rudely, we respect their life spark. Respect helps us learn about the power of harmony, focus less on ourselves, and build appreciation for the vital role of others in life—regardless of their circumstances, their background, or their sense of humor or lack thereof. It doesn't matter if a customer thinks differently than we do about a sensitive issue or has an opposite viewpoint on an area of life we think crucial: *respect is inclusive*. When we learn not to be intimidated by condescending, bossy know-it-alls, we gain greater respect for our dignity and common sense. When we balance offering someone library service—an opportunity for learning—with a "mind our own business" approach—not trying or expecting to change that person—we gain respect by our discernment and maturity. Respect allows us to forgive, tolerate, and honor others. We strive to offer opportunities through library services, activities, and content to help people draw out their best qualities for learning and growing. It helps us not to cross the line by trying to do something we cannot, such as change another person or force a perspective onto someone. When we as professional librarians apply our understanding that each member of humanity shares a common purpose to be their best—even when they don't live up to their best—we activate goodwill through respect.

The big idea of *compassion* mitigates a separative tendency and helps us to love, understand, and support customers, colleagues, and people who have opposing views from us or who come from different backgrounds. We can focus tolerance, kindness, empathy, discernment, and wisdom to help us express compassion through goodwill in order to take care of ourselves while supporting others—whether geniuses or bigots—in their lifelong learning. This helps us minimize unhelpful criticism toward others. We librarians can help ourselves and others learn to distinguish between rational analysis and irrational disapproval of what we don't like. We can reduce any tendency to be harshly critical, and instead use critical thinking skills to judge in a helpful way. At the same time, compassion does not mean that we give in or adapt to the mischief or harmfulness of others. When someone tries to poison a discussion with doubt and disharmony or aims to disparage or demean another person, or even threatens physical harm, compassion combined with discernment helps us determine how to respond in immediate and practical ways. *Compassion is not emotional goo.* It gives us a disciplined approach to life. It makes us strong, not weak. We can use compassion combined with discernment to think maturely. We can judge in constructive ways in order to help ourselves and others.

The big idea of *reverence* celebrates all that is beautiful, helpful, and right in the world, the universe—and life itself. We can start with revering our own achievements, our colleagues' successes, and our library's impact—though we should never presume that we are greater than others. Celebrating our accomplishments and those of others creates momentum for more opportunities to improve library service and contribute to enlightening humanity. Reverence is the act of identifying, pondering, and adoring big ideas—such as beauty, goodwill, and helpfulness—in order to incorporate them into our personality and enrich life. "Children—by their nature of learning through trial and error—often teach parents and caregivers to revere the deeper meaning of patience and recognize the joy of learning through mistakes," says Betsy Diamant-Cohen, executive director of Mother Goose on the Loose. When we understand that mistakes made by children or adults—or ourselves—are opportunities to learn and become a better person, we harness the power of reverence as an energy or tool with no limits. For example, no matter how confusing or staggering a situation may seem to be, *reverence for the good to be found in any problem can help solve it.* Reverence is one of the first core values or qualities to cultivate—in person, on the phone, or online—because it's easy to perceive that life sparkles with accomplishments. It is nourished throughout life via the common adage: *treat others the way you want to be treated.* Reverence helps us strengthen goodwill.

Expressed daily, *goodwill* sharpens our skills of tolerance and forgiveness. Some people believe that tolerance and forgiveness require direct confrontation. Confrontation may seem useful, but when we think things through, confrontation is quite unnecessary. For example, the act of being brutally honest contradicts goodwill. Adversarial discussions, confessions, and resolutions are not needed and may be harmful. The passion of anger, tears of sadness, and feelings of guilt can deflect us from reaching the goal and energetically project our goodwill to others. These false concepts eliminate the value of working with big ideas. Goodwill, not confrontations, is what is needed to resolve conflict.

Others assume that the act of tolerating and forgiving means that we give up and give in to injustice and corruption. On the contrary, we are not ignoring indiscretions. We are not forgiving another person's obligation to learn to act responsibly—we have no authority to do so anyway. It is not the library's job to teach them a life lesson. It is our job as library staffers to welcome everybody, including bigots, who pay their taxes or their tuition. If someone is interested in using the library, it doesn't matter what that person thinks and believes in their mind and heart, or states outside of the library. We apply and bask in the light of integrity. We mind our own business.

Wallowing in anger or disappointment—no matter how "justified" by the shortcomings of internal or external customers—does not help library service. If we engage in and practice forgiveness and tolerance toward others, we can turn our attitudes, feelings, and thoughts into powerful tools for resolving conflicts.

The big idea of goodwill is revealed in great literature and poetry. From Alexandre Dumas's *The Count of Monte Cristo* to C. S. Lewis's *The Lion, the Witch, and the Wardrobe* to Shakespeare's *Romeo and Juliet*, this universal truth affects people in a positive manner. Goodwill is a big (abstract) idea that fuels tolerance and forgiveness. Tolerance and forgiveness, in turn, activate and animate goodwill. Juliet forgives Romeo after he kills her cousin, Tybalt. When she rejects a marriage proposal by Paris, Juliet's father uses forgiveness to dissolve his anger toward her. Tolerance ultimately helps to bind the Montague and Capulet families.

HELPFULNESS

Beauty in life, such as the *best* in library service, collaborations, friendships, and art or music, does not automatically happen without the tools of goodwill, reverence, compassion, and respect. In fact, beauty is meant to be understood, built, and expressed. It is not something to just be consumed. Another tool for planting, cultivating, and expressing beauty in life is helpfulness. "I try to be helpful by offering library programs that—as a retired senior myself—I present to senior citizens about balancing online safety with the excitement and value of emerging technologies," says Hash Newman, a library volunteer for senior programming at the Carroll County (MD) Public Library. Libraries can assist customers to improve their competency with technology to help them connect socially, spark new learning, and support them with everything from paying utilities online to taking better care of their health.

By nurturing helpfulness in daily life, we discover another big idea, harmlessness—which is an *active* expression of goodwill. It helps us to avoid paying mere lip service to goodwill. Instead of revering the ideal of excellent customer service without always paying attention to customers' actual responses to desk interactions, we become skilled at exceptional service. A good place to start using the tool of harmlessness is by trying to spot any tendency to be less than cheerful with customers or colleagues.

Harm*fulness* can happen when we don't focus our cheerfulness when assisting a customer, or when we don't make needed decisions or when we avoid following through on our commitments and responsibilities. A tendency to harm someone, intentionally or not—by being unkind or by not speaking up when it's important to do so—can be curbed by paying attention.

Sometimes we don't realize that unrealistic expectations can cause hurt or confusion. For example, if we expect that the library's success depends on our customers reforming themselves or stakeholders providing compensation for past mistakes, we are holding the library hostage to the unlikely possibility that "bad people" will undergo a sudden transformation. We should make no restrictions on providing opportunities for learning for those who want to take advantage of services and opportunities. No matter if someone learns or not, we wish everyone well.

As the word *harmlessness* implies, we make it a priority to never harm another person or being—even by accident. We can harm another by not realizing that we can say too much *or* too little in response to a question. We can harm others by omitting to do something that is helpful, or by not giving a friendly acknowledgment to someone approaching the information desk while we finish another transaction.

Swift writes in "The Battle of the Books" that "although men are accused for not knowing their weakness, yet perhaps as few know their own strength." Pay attention, beautiful librarian! This is where librarians can do their best work by using goodwill and helping people recognize their inner nobility as human beings, their strengths to temper any weakness, and their potential to enjoy learning and growing throughout life.

NOTES

1. Jonathan Swift, "The Battle of the Books," p. 9, Freeditorial.com, https://freeditorial.com/en/books/the-battle-of-the-books-and-other-short-pieces/readonline.
2. Swift, "The Battle of the Books," 7.

10
Wisdom through Discernment and Courage

The Doors of Wisdom are never shut.

—BENJAMIN FRANKLIN

Our work as librarians—at all levels of library staff—is to brighten the gloomy corners of life and fill them with light. A key way to do this is by discovering and responding to the light and wisdom of universal or big ideas found in literature, poetry, music, art, and other areas of culture. For instance, we can ponder a poem by Emily Dickinson about *striving to be our best* and how that helps us to interact effectively with others and fulfill our responsibilities. We can reflect a bit more and try to grasp how the essence of the poem can strengthen our ability to express wisdom, courage, and discernment.

> We play at paste,
> Till qualified for pearl,
> Then drop the paste,
> And deem ourself a fool.
> The shapes, though, were similar,
> And our new hands
> Learned gem-tactics
> Practising sands.[1]

"Paste" is a transparent hard glass used in making artificial gemstones. Throughout history and from culture to culture, jewelry-making has included imitation or paste stones, often stunningly beautiful, but not real gemstones—which can fool us at first. Dickinson suggests that using paste stones—learning through daily activities and events—helps to develop "gem-tactics" or skills to work with the making of pearls—expressing big ideas. Fooling around with paste—doing our best to learn, grow, and contribute each day—is not wasted. Paste qualifies us to take a leap to pearl.

Libraries of all types across the spectrum may help a person seize a possibility and turn it into opportunity—for example, to learn through great poetry and then be able to understand a big idea and express it. The true role of a library is not to serve as a collection of arcane resources but to be *a repository of wisdom*. Learning to connect to big ideas and to our inner talents can act as catalysts to offer outstanding library services, collections, and activities. Only library staff can change libraries from a bunch of books, a bundle of technology, or an array of activities into a source of wisdom. In fact, libraries can offer something no other agency across the spectrum of civilization offers—*an open invitation to walk through the doors of wisdom without promoting any ideology, be it political, social, or religious.*

If the big idea of goodwill is covered in a philosophy course, it may be given lip service as something nice that Plato talked about in the abstract. "Learning to Work with Big Ideas" is not a subject in the school curriculum, but the school library or media center can invite students to explore great literature and poetry. Community groups, places of worship, and online meet-ups may discuss love, harmony, and patience—but a library can guide individuals to sources to discover how to activate these life virtues without pressure, dogma, or prescribed tenets. "Training the Mind to Embrace Truth, Beauty, and Wisdom" may not be offered at the local college—but the college library can connect people to resources to learn to think about big ideas. "Library 101: How to Enlighten Humanity" may not be in a master's program—but we library staff can take it upon ourselves to be lifelong learners and tap the wellsprings of our individuality, talent, courage, wisdom, and joy.

Wisdom is not a set of facts or theories to be memorized but a big idea to be explored, revered, and expressed. If wisdom is taught by studying Greek or Hindu philosophy, Alexander Pope, William Shakespeare, and Ralph Waldo Emerson, will students learn that they can tap the power and meaning of wisdom—or any big idea—and interpret and apply it for whatever they need each day? A great thinker constantly uses everything he knows to "up the ante" on his ability to think things through. A complete thinker does not get bogged down in new fads but instead focuses on the new currents of *inspired* thinking—and embraces them. Great thinkers and writers of the past can help us discover new ways to understand and apply wisdom and other treasures of life for now and in the future.

Wisdom is needed by a librarian to establish a helpful mindset. "Ideas" are not just something to throw around carelessly. People listen to them. Wisdom helps us learn to ponder and understand *big ideas versus small ideas*. We develop the thought structure to examine ideas by tracing them back to their original source. Does an "idea" lead to goodwill or to confusion? Does it lead to optimism or to discouragement? An "idea" can affect a person's life. A *helpful mindset* means that we listen to people, respect each customer, and help them to learn and grow at their own pace. We offer resources to help people acquire the understanding they pursue. We avoid a pedagogical approach that prescribes what "ideas" someone should or should not be learning. A *harmful mindset* means "I know better than you."

THE JOY OF DISCERNMENT

Too often, an overbearing reader badgers and pleads with fellow book club members or friends and family to think a certain way (small idea thinking). By contrast, a genial reader invites thoughtful reflection and looks for inspiration in all books (big idea thinking).

Small Idea Reader: Isn't this author saying that nothing can be done to correct the bad in society? And, don't you agree? Isn't the author clearly saying that there is no hope for the future, that we are doomed? Don't you agree? *(You've got to feel the way I do. If you don't agree, I won't respect you. If you don't agree, I won't trust you.)* What has the world come to? What are we going to do?

Big Idea Reader: Although I can understand the author's gloom-and-doom point of view—and I have certainly experienced some of the bad in society of which he writes—I'm optimistic. I saw how he ultimately wove a message of hope into the book by encouraging people to be helpful to each other. *(There is no upper ceiling of learning when it comes to activating big ideas, such as hope.)* I find that the more I treat others the way I want them to treat me—using the "golden rule" that my mother taught me—the easier it is to see the good in others, despite their flaws. I am hopeful about the future.

Jamie Naidoo, Ph.D., a professor at the University of Alabama and the president (2018–2019) of the Association for Library Service to Children, says, "Let's treat others 1,000 times better than we would want to be treated!" If a reader uses a book to lash out at others or tries to impose a belief, this negates the notion of "reading to enlighten." If a reader exploits a book by using its unhelpful ideas to chide others, his fellow book club members, friends, and family can turn that experience around for themselves and create an opportunity to learn and grow. They can use discernment to read, understand, and clarify the essence of the book. They can cheerfully hope for and invite—but not expect—the reader to ponder the nugget of hope found in the book. In the course of discussing and thinking things through, they can become aware of big ideas together, such as hope, wisdom, and courage, and integrate them into life—*finding the capacity to turn paste into pearl.*

The more we can take a book "as is," the more we can explore its essence. If the writing leads to thinking that is dull, disheartening, or depressing, is it better to stop reading? Yes, if it's going to lead to unconstructive ponderings or hurtful thoughts. Do we respond to the book by "doubling down" on our likes and dislikes? Do we use a piece of writing as an instrument for persuading, attacking, and berating others, or do we use it as a tool for learning and being inspired? If we find that the writing compels us to question and improve ourselves, then it is worthwhile. Even if a piece of writing is permeated with misinformation or the ideology of one side or another, we can often find thoughtful gems or pearls of wisdom in it.

It can be easy—for any of us—to be influenced by and fill our minds with small or misleading ideas. However, with a dollop of effort, a bit of focus, and a spark of joy, we can learn to align our thinking with universal or big ideas. We can distinguish between universal ideas and small ideas that have been so watered down as to become unhelpful and perhaps harmful. For example, a group called the Sophists in ancient Greece would argue over different topics and present false information with the goal of confusing, frightening, and angering people and thus gaining power over them. Socrates and Plato taught students how to avoid letting others do their thinking for them.

When we read a book or other piece of writing, fiction or nonfiction, we can ask a few helpful questions based on Plato's method of learning through dialogues in order to determine that book's potential wisdom or lack thereof:

- How does the writer connect us to the big ideas underlying the topic?
- Can the ideas in the book be traced back and linked to universal ideas like wisdom, beauty, courage, goodwill, or a myriad of other big ideas to inspire, uplift, and expand our thinking?
- If not, what sources do the ideas lead us toward? Is the information in the book misleading or hyperbole? Do the ideas encourage fear, doubt, anger, worry? Will they lead to mischief in our thinking? Will it be helpful *and wise* to stop reading such a book?
- *Or* does the book spark our curiosity and sense of joy, and encourage our deepest and best thoughts—even if it's only a pearl or two of wisdom within a jumble of misinformation?
- How can we welcome big ideas like a gracious host and entertain them in our mind for a friendly, warmhearted, and lively dinner party?
- What do the big ideas reveal to us that can expand our awareness and understanding of life, including seeing where our current thinking may be misguided or even hoodwinked?

The Sophist approach—to deceive, dispirit, disquiet, and befuddle—dominates today's political atmosphere, with each political party playing off the other. By asking a few right questions and making an effort to ponder, we can discover that cleverness dominates the debate, not wisdom. No matter if it's to the left, right, or down the middle—disorientation, not clarity, is a result. When we are pressured by Sophist-types to think a certain way, whether in the political, social, or religious realms, we can lessen their influence by using discernment, mental courage, and joy to help ourselves and better serve our library users.

The goal is to read for discovery and revelation with a discerning mind. Reading the words of a book or essay is a first step. Reading between the lines is a second step to explore hidden meanings. If the writing is worthwhile and expands our mind, we are now reading above the lines. We can connect and express big ideas, reject any foolish or unhelpful concepts, and add value to our thinking. When we engage our minds with imaginative fiction, insightful essays, powerful nonfiction, and astute biographies, we are *reading to enlighten ourselves. Learning and growing to expand our mind has no ceiling or upper limit.*

THE COURAGE TO GET PEOPLE FLYING (ENLIGHTENED)

By expanding our ability to be aware, curious, and to think, we strengthen our understanding to use library resources to promote wisdom. It is never enough for a library staff member today to just be helpful and compassionate—discernment and courage are important as well. The tool of discernment can help us locate the wellsprings of big ideas as we read, enjoy music and art, and ponder how to translate these ideas into productive library service and activities.

The bridges that libraries are building to big ideas—through their resources and activities—require strong building blocks, including courage. "It takes some daring to make it a priority to listen to library users and non-users alike. This means the library doesn't just offer the occasional paper or online survey to get some feedback, but builds relationships with people. It takes savviness to respect our customers to find their own path," says Catherine Hakala-Ausperk, library instructor, consultant, and author of *Build a Great Team: One Year to Success*.

Courage and intelligent risk-taking are needed not only to find universal or big ideas but to comprehend and apply them in life. For example, during the Revolutionary War, an American officer suddenly appeared on his horse in the woods where a British sharpshooter was stationed. When their eyes met, the officer was unable to quickly pull out his pistol to defend himself and simply stared down the soldier. The soldier did not fire his rifle. The American officer cantered away and avoided getting shot. That officer was George Washington.

Washington handled the moment with *strength of heart or courage* and escaped probable death.

While many librarians value efficiency, far too many of us tend to be perfectionists who insist on being fully prepared before making a major decision or launching a new idea. As a result, we may revert to focusing on the short term and avoid taking sufficient time to reflect and plan for the long term. The unintended outcome can be a missed opportunity to recognize when the tides are in favor of library innovation and change.

The rising tide of change drives issues into the open. We need to be adaptable and optimistic in order to explore and discover what works and what doesn't work. Can we be ready to act? If yes, it's possible to soar ahead in a short period of time.

A good example of openness comes to us from the airline industry. Key leaders in the commercial airline industry of the 1930s were poised to make major improvements in safety, comfort, speed, and affordability. After the fiery disaster of the "lighter-than-air" *Hindenburg* airship in 1937, the competition between the smooth-floating, quiet, and tranquil "zeppelins" and the rough-flying, noisy, and stomach-churning "aeroplanes" ended in favor of the latter. Improvement in speeds increased the attraction of airplane technology as well—by the mid-1930s, airplane speed could reach 200 mph compared to a zeppelin's top speed of 85 mph. A trip from London to New York covering about 3,500 miles by zeppelin could take two to three days. By airplane it could take less than 20 hours. Traveling by airplane today with an average speed of 560 miles from New York to London, it takes only 6.2 hours to arrive.

Eddie Rickenbacker, the founder and president of Eastern Airlines, helped to transform airplane travel. Given the limited technology of the 1920s and 1930s, planes would drop hundreds of feet in a matter of moments because of extreme turbulence. Activities such as eating, walking about, and using the lavatory were conducted at the passengers' own risk. Suppressing nausea and vomiting was a priority. The first women to serve in the airline stewardess role were professional nurses. But over time, the airplane went from an incredibly grueling way to get from one city to another—with frequent stops for fueling and emergency landings due to mechanical problems—to a faster, safer, more affordable and comfortable experience.

Rickenbacker was poised and ready to take advantage of the mounting tide of air travel progress. He got his team behind the mantra "get people flying," and began solving issues like making air travel less subject to turbulence. Eastern quickly became the most successful airline company and maintained its number-one status for decades.

"I like to tell the story of my father and his colleagues who built zeppelins in the early twentieth century. Although the promise of lighter-than-air technology was not fulfilled and ended in the *Hindenburg* fire disaster, it helped pave the way for the airplane—a heavier-than-air craft—to become a safer, faster, and more commercially viable form of air transport," says Horst Schirmer, a physician at Johns Hopkins and a speaker at libraries, schools, and colleges. Dr. Schirmer was only six years old when he flew on a *Hindenburg* test flight. He added, "A dirigible was like a luxurious ocean liner in the air but calmer, without any seasickness movements. Lighter-than-air transport had the capability to stay afloat when an engine stopped working, allowing for an opportunity to repair the engine in the air, unlike with the airplane. Air travel by dirigible centered on the adventure of floating in the air, and the aerodynamics design used to interweave a gracefulness unsurpassed in other transportation modes. It was a joy to experience."

FIGURE 10.1

Libraries are in the midst of great change. After the era of lighter-than-air travel of the early twentieth century, the new, emerging airline industry picked up the mantle to get people flying and carried it forward to establish safe, comfortable commercial air flight. Either we, library staff, renew our commitment to pick up and carry the mantle forward—to enlighten humanity—for generations to come or libraries will become a thing of the past, like the zeppelin airship industry.

This work is in the public domain in the United States because it is a work prepared by an officer or employee of the U.S. government as part of that person's official duties under the terms of Title 17, Chapter 1, Section 105 of the U.S. Code.

"I've watched dozens of firms have it both ways. They transformed them-selves into better organizations for the future [with long-term planning] and they provided good results quarter by quarter [with short-term planning]," writes John P. Kotter, author of *Leading Change*.[2] If we integrate big ideas into our thinking and activities, we can develop an intuitive sense of timing. We will be prepared to align our decisions and activities with the ideal moment in time—for both the short term and the long term.

The courage to trust in right timing is invaluable. We can look for interconnected possibilities that make us aware of a new opportunity on the horizon; for example, forming a new collaboration or revising an old one. If a mistake or misunderstanding comes into play between partners, it's something to be celebrated in the sense of using it as an opportunity to revise, refresh, and reinvent the collaboration. We become attracted to the collaboration and the chance to launch something new or make improvements. Hope supersedes any misunderstanding with a partner and helps drive the momentum to work together.

Technology learning is forcing libraries to change. More importantly, the issue of narrow thinking—or the "react first, think later" approach—needs our attention, focus, and wisdom. Are we ready to overcome our stubbornness or hesitancy and find solutions to the tendency of humankind to overreact and not think things through? Can we accept that libraries are designed to become a major part of those solutions—and rejoice in our role? Are we ready to be optimistic and confident that we'll figure things out? How should we revise our priorities and efforts?

Librarians can *nurture the awareness and application of courage, discernment, and wisdom.* Courage is required to take intelligent risks. Discernment helps us let go of worn-out beliefs, revise our thinking, and improve our efficiency. Rickenbacker's ability to understand the overarching purpose of his industry helped tap the wisdom behind long-term transportation goals and the courage to "get people flying" in the short term. The overarching purpose of libraries is nothing less than to enlighten humanity. Intelligent risk-taking can help us find our courage and willingness to ride the rising tide of change for libraries.

Our duty is to hook customers up with books and resources that contain big ideas. By listening to people, we can help them get to big ideas that contain the answers and insights they are seeking. It is not our duty to convince them what to explore or think. The authors—of books and other resources—will do the convincing. We need courage to listen to users and non-users alike to help them get to the big ideas. Otherwise, they may not get to explore and activate concepts such as goodwill, respect, integrity, optimism, and resilience.

The librarian has a golden opportunity to keep the doors of wisdom open and poised for people to walk through them. Courage, mental toughness, gracefulness, and joy are required daily to provide the right resources and activities for the needs and wants of users and non-users. It's time to "get people enlightened." This important work cannot be done by librarians alone, but we—*unlike any other agency in civilization*—oversee the portal for lifelong learning and expressing big ideas. *Librarians hold the key to making sure that Franklin's Doors of Wisdom stay open for everyone to become the best person they can be.*

NOTES

1. Emily Dickinson, *The Complete Works of Emily Dickinson: Published as They Were Written, with Very Few and Superficial Changes* (SMK Books – Kindle Version, 2014), Location 268.
2. John P. Kotter, *Leading Change* (Boston: Harvard Business School Press, 1996), 125.

PART IV

Finding the Light within Ideas

11

Curiosity

Be less curious about people
and more curious about ideas.

—MARIE CURIE

The mind is not meant to be idle, rigid, or stagnant. Nor is it designed to be "schooled," "educated," or pressured to become "well-read"—and then let loose into the wilds of unenlightened and sloppy thinking. It is meant to tap the power of the life-force—the light within big ideas.

In this chapter we'll explore what it means to be a lifelong learner and *an agent of big ideas*. We'll not only seek an understanding of an idea, but also learn to penetrate its hidden meaning. As library staffers, if we don't yet think of ourselves as agents of universal ideas, how about acknowledging that we are each meant to take on and grow into that role? We are meant to be loving, creative human beings with the capacity to turn any and every situation into an unexpected opportunity to learn and reach a new plateau of mature thinking. We are meant to enrich life by being courageous thinkers.

As thinkers, we should be willing to recognize and accept that events in life—no matter whether we view them as "good" or "bad"—are opportunities for learning. We may not like it when milk spills on the floor or when someone drives through a stop sign and hits our car, but we have choices in how to respond. We can respond with anger and frustration or with goodwill and thoughtfulness. "When you react with anger, you can't make an intelligent decision," says Katya Vogt, the global lead for media and information literacy initiatives at IREX, a global development and education organization. How we think and act in each situation determines how much or how little we learn. Often what seems at first like a "bad" experience turns out in the long run to be a good one. For example, suppose a colleague doesn't follow through with a commitment. If we become agitated and are unable to forgive that person—a reaction—we are not learning from the experience. However, if we try to understand the workload and pressures on our colleagues, seek to appreciate their perspectives, and recognize that they are doing their best in that moment—a proactive response—we may be able to better handle any situation and forgive others, allowing us to move on. And in moving beyond the event, we are able to strengthen a positive bond with the person and together be more productive in the future. When we approach experiences and "events of life"—no matter how unpleasant or uncomfortable—*with a proactive response, we are better able to discover the kernel of insight in them to help us learn.*

For example, we may revere the notion of "peace," but seldom activate it. Can we use peace to transform reactions—not just the other person's but ours too—when someone is angry with us? We can penetrate beyond our general understanding of our colleague or library customer to an inner design that gives meaning to their life. The golden rule of treating others in ways we'd like to be treated helps us learn to activate the big idea of peace.

We can transform ignorance into wisdom and unhappiness into joyfulness. When a person behaves immaturely or if we behave less than our best, we can use the big idea of maturity to transform ineffective reactions—not just ours but the other person's too—into harm*less*ness and helpfulness. We do this through finding the light or penetrating the meaning of big ideas.

During the Carnegie Foundation's library construction grant program from 1889 to 1919—which built more than 1,600 libraries in the United States alone—Andrew Carnegie did not ask for naming rights. His only request was to post the phrase "Let There Be Light" above the entrance to signify the library as a cultural institution pursuing the enlightenment of humanity. Library staffers can take these words to heart by activating this motto. We can seek out the light to help clients solve the puzzles of life.

Artists, composers, novelists, architects, and filmmakers challenge us to penetrate the mysteries of life when they demonstrate through their creative labors the multidimensional aspects of life. Many levels of meaning in life are documented by all those who participate in creating culture. We librarians are poised by the nature of our role to be enormously helpful in using and studying the many branches of culture. We can learn to interact and honor the light they represent. For example, reading outstanding literature and nonfiction can train and open the mind to look for new perspectives. Science fiction and fantasy help us perceive the interconnectivity of designs and patterns. Excellent fiction builds a well-focused imagination and an intuitive ability to see the big picture. Essays can offer profound insights into human nature and communicate big ideas to a cross-section of readers. Great essayists for consideration include Ralph Waldo Emerson, Michel de Montaigne, and Sir Francis Bacon. A well-written piece of humor or satire can help us detach from our assumptions and explore new mental territory in order to update and massage our thinking. We can spark curiosity in ourselves and others to think like a detective to solve the mysteries of life—to think multidimensionally.

CALL TO ACTION

A common antidote to any reluctance or resistance to learning is to develop a strong desire to learn. The library's role is to help people learn to find the light within an idea so that they can tap its power. We cannot afford to be only partly filled with curiosity. Many libraries approach services and activities with a preconceived notion rather than consulting the light within big ideas such as optimism, wisdom, beauty, and patience. It is only by tapping the forces of these ideas that the purpose of the library to enlighten humanity can be fulfilled.

Another tool is viewing the world as a place that is mostly caring and full of goodwill—promoting the practice of looking for and drawing out the good in others. Libraries of all types across the spectrum are ideal for helping people to be curious and learn how to penetrate the big idea of goodwill, express its riches, and redeem the imperfections we encounter. It is common to blame, complain, avoid, or become agitated and defensive. By recognizing the practical energy of forgiveness, we can tap the power of goodwill to help dissolve the feeling of harm. We can get on with the more important things in life—being the best librarians we can be and helping our customers be their best. Forgiveness and tolerance may not always be easy to apply. By taking challenges in stride, however, we can stay focused on our work. The ghost of Prince Hamlet's deceased father in Shakespeare's tragedy counsels his son about his mother's bad behavior:

> But howsoever thou pursuest this act,
>
> Taint not thy mind, nor let thy soul contrive
>
> Against thy mother aught. Leave her to heaven
>
> And to those thorns that in her bosom lodge
>
> To prick and sting her.[1]

Hamlet, of course, ignores this advice and causes a great deal of grief, tragedy, and bloody death. Leaving retribution to the afterlife is not easy to learn, but the ability to forgive and harness the power of goodwill frees us to pursue creative, practical opportunities. Are we too much like Hamlet, thinking that we must bring retribution that is better left to others? As Alexander Pope said, "To err is human; to forgive, divine."[2] If we move on, we can more easily focus on our professional and domestic goals with grace and serenity. Forgiveness and goodwill help remove barriers to our growth and promote equilibrium in all that we do.

However, another instrument in our librarian toolkit is *curiosity*. The skill of curiosity can help build the bridge to the big ideas of wisdom, goodwill, and others to replace deformed ideas such as blame, worry, and anger. "What parts of ourselves do we bring to the framing of our tasks and relationships—the worried, anxious, and doubting parts or the creative, caring, curious parts?" asks author and educator Faith Rogow, Ph.D. Curiosity can help the mind stay busy to get things done. *Intelligent curiosity leads to intelligent activity.*

Curiosity is a tenacious and joyful quest—a call to action—for expanding our awareness in order to become more effective in life. It has several levels, from unproductive and perhaps harmful to mature, inspiring, and magnificent. Curiosity is meant to help us learn as much as we can about life and to grow as human beings. The lower levels are based in an unhelpful, emotional reactiveness, such as gossiping and snooping. This type of curiosity can lead to becoming too "involved"—and getting into trouble or inviting grief—in situations where minding one's own business is a better course of action. The higher levels can be described as a focused, intelligent curiosity. It invokes discovery, sees through disinformation, neutralizes mental fatigue, increases our options, and activates our creativity.

A higher-level—or intelligent—curiosity pays tribute to silence. It is useful to learn to maintain silence and the skill of minding one's own business. A library staff member's role is to guide, not dictate. The genius of library service is letting each person find his or her own way.

Intelligent curiosity challenges our assumptions about all things in life. Unlike the lower levels of curiosity—gossiping and snooping—intelligent curiosity does not reinforce our prejudices, but shatters them. The enemy of intelligent thinking is the myriad assumptions we make about everything!

We can serve customers and students far beyond what we can currently imagine—if we encourage people to find the answers themselves. Libraries fuel curiosity. When a person asks a question, the library has the answer and points that person in the right direction. However, the key is for people to find and examine the answer on their own. For example, how can we learn to turn reactiveness into a discerning response when watching a news story? Did we respond emotionally, stirring up pockets of biases? Was the story newsworthy or sensational? Did we notice a deeper message about life? Did the story reveal arrogance and insult or achievement and brilliance? Has it inspired us to reform and grow?

We assume that the library is worth supporting by a tax levy, school budget, or university foundation allocation, but if a student or patron asks a question that a librarian cannot answer or doesn't think she should answer, why should the funder support the library? Libraries are stagnant until someone asks a question. We want to be a magnet for a person's need to know, inquire, *and grow*. Libraries can get busy vivifying and invigorating the quality of big ideas when people ask questions.

Because the vast majority of individuals are literate today and most have access to online information, we need to be more curious about the purpose of a library. Maybe the library's potential to enlighten humanity, such as helping individuals discover and explore big ideas, will earn it a place of reverence in each community, school, and college like never before—instead of an institution to be cut or downsized. Library staffers can become role models for how to tap into and express big ideas, endure challenges without becoming depressed or resentful, forgive indignities while maintaining grace and integrity, and express wisdom in actual—not theoretical—situations.

For example, Benjamin Franklin tapped a high level of curiosity throughout his long life. By the time he died in 1790, his curiosity had led him to many pursuits, accomplishments, discoveries, and inventions. Franklin's long-lasting achievements sparked by his lifelong curiosity include the following:

- His wisdom and wit during the founding era of the United States
- The establishment of the University of Pennsylvania, one of the preeminent institutions of higher education in the United States
- The founding of the American Philosophical Society, which celebrated its 275th anniversary in 2018 sponsoring scholars and research
- Public lending libraries
- Fire departments
- Hospitals
- Post offices
- Paper currency
- His experiments, speculations, and hunches in the areas of electricity, oceanography, geology, and meteorology—helping to guide others to correct his mistakes and expand upon these fields of study
- Bifocals
- Daylight savings time
- Letter copier
- Lightning rod
- His autobiography, written as a letter to his son about tuning into and expressing the big ideas of life
- His timeless and universal ability to create right human relationships using goodwill, humor, and integrity

Andrew Carnegie's motto "Let There Be Light" is a call to action for librarians to seek enlightenment in order to fulfill the library's purpose to illumine humanity. Curiosity, when properly focused, penetrates the ideal design for all aspects of life. The library's role in civilization is designed to bring out our best in order to figure out how to learn, grow, and serve our communities beyond what we—or they—can image. *Whenever we grow first*, we inspire others. A library cannot grow without inspiring others to do so too—including the library staff as well as patrons.

Are we curious? Or do we accept what the "experts" say is true without holding them accountable? Does it make it right if someone demands privacy yet denies another person their privacy? How much do the "experts" know? We can use Plato's helpful method of inquiry to challenge our assumptions and question, well, just about everything. This process can lead us to trace a big idea back to its source: "Once more, from the beginning!" For example, the big idea of freedom can be traced back to its kernel—to think for oneself. The big idea of freedom—or thinking for oneself—cannot be fragmented into differing political views. Many positive insights inspire the major American political parties, but thinking for oneself is universal, inspirational, and above politics—the way libraries can be when they are at their best.

THE CURIOSITY SHOP

The adage "As we think in our heart, so we are," is worth reflecting upon. At first glance, we may think it defines the power and right application of thinking. When we can trace it back to the original (in Greek, Hebrew, and Latin), we learn there is more to this saying: "As we think in our heart, so we are; Eat and drink, says he to thee; but his heart is not with thee." We discover the message that many people base their thinking not on informed consideration, but on emotion and belief that lacks a solid basis in the facts. A person may say something or pretend to be curious, but not mean it. "I want to be curious, but not *that* curious." The higher levels of curiosity can uncover suggestions and evidence of one's unhelpful assumptions, for example.

We want to be free to guide our own thinking and help others do the same. By questioning our assumptions and seeking to discover the truth, we can discern the value of the higher phases of curiosity. In doing so, we can connect with big ideas regularly and train the mind to be alive with the highest levels of curiosity. In addition, how can librarians help others direct their curiosity toward a healthy inquiry about big ideas? If, for example, we focus a great deal of our attention on what is happening in Washington, D.C., right now, it can produce agitation. Instead, we can "keep it light" by appreciating and honoring those noble and beautiful souls who are part of the effort to make politics work and help government be its best. We can stay above the fray of politics. When someone gets absorbed in la-la-Hollywood-land, it can quickly become an uninspired and dissatisfying gossipy experience. We can focus, instead, on the learning and inspiration to be derived from good movies.

In Charles Dickens's novel *The Old Curiosity Shop*, Mrs. Jarley of Jarley's wax-work show says, "I won't go so far as to say, that, as it is, I've seen wax-work quite like life, but I've certainly seen some life that was exactly like wax-work." Intelligent curiosity—not the busybody or snooping level—can keep the mind from stagnating into a wax-work frame of thinking.

FIGURE 11.1

C. H. Graves, *Old Curiosity Shop, London* ca. 1900, Philadelphia.

Photograph: Retrieved from the Library of Congress, https://www.loc.gov/item/2003675312/

Are we reading great thinkers, listening to great composers, and pondering the ideas of big idea explorers who have stretched their thinking to help pave the way for us and our customers? Do we read Plato, Shakespeare, and Dickens—joyously even when it can be slow going? Do we ponder Yogananda and Emerson—regularly? Do we tune in to Mozart and Vivaldi—triumphantly as they were meant to be experienced? Or do we only read romance novels?

We can tap the force of big ideas when we read, study, listen, and ponder the greats. Some people only give lip service to universal ideas. They like what a big idea conveys, but they don't apply it or express it in their work and domestic duties. Ooey gooey cake has its place as a yummy dessert, but it's easy for us to get trapped in pursuing a feel-good sensation in life that leads to nothing permanent or long-term. The problem with "feel-good" is that it cannot be sustained; it is based on sheer emotion and not on thinking. The more we learn to think completely and thoroughly, the more we learn that emotions are meant to enrich and express big ideas, not impose them on others.

THE GOSSAMER THREAD

When we apply curiosity to a poem such as Walt Whitman's "A Noiseless Patient Spider," we gain insights into connecting with the inspiration and light within big ideas:

> A noiseless patient spider,
>
> I mark'd where on a little promontory it stood isolated,
>
> Mark'd how to explore the vacant vast surrounding,
>
> It launch'd forth filament, filament, filament, out of itself,
>
> Ever unreeling them, ever tirelessly speeding them.
>
> And you O my soul where you stand,
>
> Surrounded, detached, in measureless oceans of space,
>
> Ceaselessly musing, venturing, throwing, seeking the spheres to
>   connect them,
>
> Till the bridge you will need be form'd, till the ductile anchor hold,
>
> Till the gossamer thread you fling catch somewhere, O my soul.[3]

We can create a bridge to the forces of big ideas—joy, wisdom, harmony, integrity, goodwill, reverence, respect—by using a gossamer thread (thinking) that gets stronger over time. If our work is suited to libraries—knowing this is our place to contribute—then we are likely to be surprised by our readiness for what we thought possible.

We should all be looking to catch and strengthen the gossamer threads of life—inspired thinking. Higher intelligence flings gossamer threads to us all the time—through great poetry, literature, science, music, art, movies, architecture, and technology. Higher intelligence also gives inspirational opportunities through our satisfying relationships with friends, family, colleagues, and customers. It flings gossamer threads through excellence in business, work, and personal projects, as well as while gardening or even washing the dishes. We may not catch them all, but there is inspiration and light within each thread. Curiosity's purpose is to fix on that light within in order to understand big ideas. It helps turn the wheels of our creativity to put the ideas into action.

Each of us may not yet contemplate how we can direct and integrate our big idea insights into the glory of serving the community. However, we can get busy with this unending joyous pursuit of applying respect and patience and harmony even when it isn't easy to do so.

Are we constantly asking our customers, what more can the library do for you? How can we act like a detective and reach beyond our expected thinking and, as much as possible, ask: hmmm? How can we be at the ready to forgive someone (even ourselves) after a faux pas? How can we avoid the temptation to ease up on the pursuit of an uplifting life? How can we make life closer to what it is meant to be—learning, growing, and serving? How can we be exceptional librarians?

A mind that is curious can get into a habit of seeking—and even demanding—answers and insights. At the same time, the curious mind accepts that there are some things we don't understand. Thinking is the ability to tap the power of a big idea without needing to know all the details of how it works. For example, we can drive a car to get us to work or the store, but we don't have to understand the workings of the internal combustion engine. We keep our food cold by using a refrigerator, but we don't need to understand how the compressor raises the pressure of the refrigerant vapors, pushing them into the coils. A mind that is charged with intelligent curiosity can understand the essence of a big idea to capture its meaning. As we focus on the potential of the idea, we gain creative insights—not concrete details—into how to reproduce it in our thinking and actions.

Intelligent curiosity helps us become explorers and enjoy the adventure of life. It breaks down the limitations of focusing too much on details or on pettiness. "Do we sometimes become overly focused on problems that we overlook solutions?" asks Tamar Sarnoff, Ph.D., branch chief of the Maryland State Library. Other stumbling blocks to curiosity that we should try to avoid are stubbornness, tunnel vision, and a lack of discernment. Each big idea has a power or force that can help us reveal its meaning and implement it. Library staff can use curiosity to wander among all the possibilities for insights and solutions in order to find the best one. We can help our constituents learn to penetrate the power of ideas by helping them develop their strength of curiosity.

NOTES

1. William Shakespeare, The Complete Works Online, *Hamlet*, act 1, scene 5, http://shakespeare.mit.edu/hamlet/hamlet.1.5.html.
2. Alexander Pope, *An Essay on Criticism: Part 2,* Poetry Foundation, https://www.poetry foundation.org/poems/44897/an-essay-on-criticism-part-2.
3. Walt Whitman, "A Noiseless Patient Spider," Poetry Foundation, https://www.poetryfoundation.org/poems/45473/a-noiseless-patient-spider.

12

Joy, Humility, and Unity

Success and happiness lie in you. Resolve to keep
happy, and your joy and you shall form an invincible
host against difficulties.
— HELEN KELLER

Celebrating ideas brings their presence into the library and helps
enlighten the library's constituency—whether individually or as a group
or community. The word *enlighten* can be traced back to earlier languages
that historians may have overlooked to describe a source of light, brightness,
joy, and delight. Enlightenment expands our natural and acquired capacities
to be our best.

Few people know how to fully express joy, practice humility, or effectively
promote unity—three big ideas that are instrumental to library service and its
overarching purpose to enlighten humanity. Many people even pretend that
these ideas don't exist or just ignore them. However, these and other big ideas
are meant to be celebrated and explored. Libraries—located in rural, subur-
ban, and urban areas, as well as schools, colleges, and other institutions—can
help activate and sustain the rising quality of the mind. The rising mind can
help infuse big ideas into all aspects of life, including the routine of daily activities. Libraries can help nurture the mind to rise above the ordinary. A good
place to start is reading what the great writers and thinkers have discovered
about the higher reaches of life. Librarians can learn to read above the lines,
not just in between the lines.

As we ponder on joy, humility, and unity, we can tap, understand, and activate their intangible essence. As a result, they help us do our work with less effort, inspire a sense of core values to guide service, and increase our ability to stay above the fray of political, social, religious, and other sensitive issues in the course of our decision-making. Without joy the mind is rather lifeless—because it can't enjoy life! A mind without humility thinks it knows it all, whereas with inspired humility we can become aware of the decent, dignified, and honorable qualities within each of us. A mind without unity is prone to emptiness and superficiality, whereas with unity the mind seeks cooperation with others and demonstrates unselfishness and understanding.

Libraries across the spectrum can be the go-to spot to help people discover resources to explore big ideas and raise the quality of their projects, skills, and accomplishments. "My parents, who did not have formal education, took me to the public library because that's how they thought I'd learn whatever I needed to learn. It was a place where there was never anything out of reach and everything was within possibility. The library promoted the joy of learning as a keynote for life," says Heidi Daniel, president and CEO of the Enoch Pratt Free Library in Baltimore.

Joy, humility, and unity—as well as tolerance, harmony, and integrity—may seem to be out of reach because they are not visible but rather "intangible" forces of life. These big ideas, however, are accessible. They can be explored and are meant to be put to use. For example, the joy of learning continues to expand throughout humanity with the increasing interest in entrepreneurship and technology and the rejuvenation of Shakespeare and opera.

Big ideas lead us to abstract thought and the rising mind. Big ideas don't put us down but lift us up in order to read above the lines to understand the wisdom, goodness, and potential within ourselves, others, and humanity. The ultimate role of the librarian is not to put people down or make them feel stupid or out-of-step with humanity, but to help lift them up.

The poet and satirist Alexander Pope described drinking deeply from the Pierian wellspring of inspired learning and thinking, referring to the ancient Greek metaphorical source (the Muses) of knowledge and inspiration: *A little learning is a dangerous thing; Drink deep, or taste not the Pierian spring.*[1] We come to know that although they may be intangible, joy, humility, and unity are available to anyone and are meant to be active. We can learn to think through how to apply them. We can tap and use their energy best if we take the time to "drink deep" and penetrate their power to help the mind rise.

By quoting Emily Dickinson in her poem "I Never Saw a Moor," we can ponder the value of the invisible, the intangible, the big ideas in life:

> I never saw a moor,
>
> I never saw the sea;
>
> Yet know I how the heather looks,
>
> And what a wave may be.

FIGURE 12.1

The Muses of Inspiration Hail the Spirit, the Messenger of Light, by Pierre Puvis de Chavannes. Painted for the Boston Public Library in 1896. Enlightenment, a winged figure, above the doorway to Bates Hall, helps connect us to the joy of learning and the light of inspiration. The figures of Study (left of the doorway) and Contemplation (right of the doorway) promote the joy of pondering and intelligent curiosity.

Information and learning activities offered with a welcoming attitude by knowledgeable, caring experts are an excellent foundation, but *libraries can only become a great treasure if we connect people with the intangible essence of big ideas. For example, the core meaning of optimism, wisdom, dignity, or any other big idea can transform a life.* The qualities of the inner essence of wisdom include clarity, genius, and achievement—as opposed to confusion, mediocrity, and idleness. The essence or intangible qualities of wisdom can give us a broader perspective on personal problems and the issues that confront humanity. It takes effort by each individual to read, study, ponder, and activate the intangibles of big ideas. Libraries are a magnificent place for books and resources with big ideas, but until individuals seek out our resources to read, ponder, and connect to these intangibles, a library is just a collection of books and resources, interesting activities, and pleasant staff.

Three of the most significant intangibles are joy, humility, and unity. They are outstanding examples of big ideas that can enhance the work of the library.

JOY

Joy adds a sparkle, lifting life out of the mundane. Joy is not to be confused with happiness, which is a pleasant, but temporary, state of contentment. For example, an Orioles fan is happy and "feels good" when his baseball team beats the White Sox. Joy is much more powerful than happiness. Joy is not a feeling, but a universal quality and mental energy expressed through activity.

Happiness can only be repeated each time favorable circumstances—which are out of our control—present themselves.

Joy is the delight in genuine accomplishment and achievement, no matter how large or small or whether through oneself, a group, or humanity. Humanity has a constant need for the universal energy of joy. It can be tapped on a regular basis.

Joy should fill the mind. It is a sure sign that we are thinking with big ideas. The library in all its interactions can help people discover the treasures held within its walls—and by doing so it can bring people joy. Joy is a healing and motivating force that is meant to be tapped and developed. When we are immersed in our activities, it helps us to step back to see alternatives. Joy can be a tool to boost uninspired or aimless moments into a realm of creativity and productivity. Joy exalts us!

By exploring another great thinker, Helen Keller, we can learn about connecting to joy and how to trace the idea of joy back to its source—the abstract or higher level of thinking. After a high fever, Keller lost her eyesight and hearing at nineteen months. She changed from a joyful toddler to a child filled with anger, confusion, and pessimism. Through the efforts of Keller's parents, Anne Sullivan, an instructor at the Perkins School for the Blind in Boston and visually impaired herself, was asked to take on the role of governess. Keller was six years old at the time and was wild, rude, and joyless. Sullivan tried tapping "sign language" letters and words onto Keller's hand. After a few weeks, Sullivan tapped out the word "water" at the water pump. In that moment, a burst of understanding—and joy—was revealed to Keller about words and language.

Keller not only learned to communicate with others but continued to use her mind to think and express big ideas. She was the first blind and deaf person in the United States to graduate from college, attending Radcliffe College at Harvard University. She dedicated herself to causes such as the American Foundation for the Blind and became a surprisingly productive and active person and a prolific writer. She continues to inspire people around the world who have heard of her and read her books.

In business terms, we can train the mind to think with reason (not emotion) and develop skills to think both from the 10,000-foot view and from the ground. It was from this higher level of thinking that six-year-old Helen Keller grasped—in a flash at the water pump—the concept of words, language, and conversation, thereby making sense of what she had been unable to see or hear.

HUMILITY

Humility is distorted a great deal. Many people may practice false humility by thinking "that's above my pay grade," or they practice false pride, which negates the dignity and nobility of our character within. Inspired humility allows us to work with big ideas.

Through vanity (boasting and conceit), we pretend to have done something worthwhile. Through a sense of unworthiness, we keep our inadequacies and limitations at the forefront, thereby denying our competence and creativity. Inspired humility works hand in hand with genuine pride to help us realize who we are, what we can do, and the value of life.

"The waving of the boughs in the storm, is new to me and old. It takes me by surprise, and yet is not unknown. Its effect is like that of a higher thought or a better emotion coming over me, when I deemed I was thinking justly or doing right,"[2] writes Ralph Waldo Emerson in his essay *Nature*. Richard Louv, an author and journalist, says, "Nature presents the young [and all ages] with something so much greater than they are; it offers an environment where they can easily contemplate infinity and eternity."[3] Inspired humility is the response to the awe of life and the beauty of nature.

Inspired humility—not false or distorted humility—focuses on the positive aspects of life. Using humility helps us *think well of ourselves and others without over- or under-estimating our abilities*. It gives us a sense of worth and personal honor in the moment-to-moment activity of life.

In Alexander Pope's "An Epistle to Burlington: Of False Taste," the fourth essay or poem of the *Moral Essays*, he describes how a person of wealth can never purchase genius or taste. The lord or owner of an estate may be able to afford a beautifully designed home, an elaborate garden, and a large private library, but he builds the house, changes the landscape, and collects books for the wrong (vain) reasons.

> Something there is more needful than Expense,
>
> And something previous e'en to Taste – 'tis Sense;
>
> Good sense, which is only the gift of heav'n

Collecting books, for example, becomes an aimless focus (false taste) instead of carefully selecting and studying books to understand them (exquisite sense of taste). *We are meant to use taste and common sense to select and read books that lead us to the intangibles or big ideas in life.* Instead, some people try to fill up their bookshelves—even using painted books of wood on the top shelves—in an attempt to impress others. However, without *the sense of taste,* the books lose their power, wholeness, and grace.

To understand Pope's references in his poem, a few terms and definitions from the art of bookbinding in the fourteenth through seventeenth centuries may be helpful. *Aldus* Manutius (c. 1449–1515) was an Italian scholar and publisher of ancient Greek philosophical texts; *Du Sueil* describes a delicate and intricately designed book cover style; *Vellum* was the name for smooth and durable animal skin used as parchment for books.

> His *Study?* with what Authors is it stored?
>
> In Books, not Authors, curious is my Lord;
>
> To all their *dated Backs* he turns you round:

These *Aldus* printed, those *Du Sueil* has bound.

Lo, some are *Vellum,* and the rest are good

For all his Lordship knows, but they are Wood.

By applying taste, common sense, and a dollop of humility, we can better focus our attention on the big ideas of life.

In his autobiography, Benjamin Franklin describes how he worked on several attributes or big ideas all his life and mastered many of them. His notation to himself in regard to humility was to "imitate Jesus and Socrates." He reports on his progress: "I struggled with humility . . . you will see it, perhaps, often in this history; for even if I could conceive that I had completely overcome it, I should probably be proud of my humility."[4]

UNITY

As there are forces of joy and humility in life to penetrate and express, there is a bigger sphere for the force of unity. Unity embraces the dignity of humanity. It helps us recognize the common hopes and aspirations among ourselves and other people and our shared strengths and achievements.

Instead of encouraging separation between different groups, the library promotes collaboration and unity. Librarians invest time and effort, for example, in designing and implementing meeting room policies to *balance a "welcome all" approach without endorsing one group over another.*

Alexander Pope describes the importance of training the mind to go back to the Pierian wellspring of learning and inspiration as a source of continuous hope, optimism, and enrichment. Pope's insights further help us explore the concept of unity. In his "Essay on Man," he says that humanity "must rise from individual to whole."

What does it mean to rise from individual to whole? It teaches each one of us to respect every individual in humankind—no matter a person's political party, gender, race, education, income, sexual orientation, skin color, background, country of origin, spiritual belief, or level of achievement. Working with the big idea of unity helps us grasp that by dint of discovering the big idea of unity within ourselves, we discover its power within humanity.

New and emerging technologies have the capacity to catch the flavor of unity and help build a bridge among individuals within an organization, across a campus, or around the world. "The potential of technology is exciting to not only help make life more convenient, but also to bring people together to create a new level of connected teaching and learning," says Bob Kuntz, director of operations and innovation at the Carroll County (MD) Public Library. Brian Zelip, an emerging technologies librarian at the Health Sciences & Human Services Library of the University of Maryland, Baltimore, adds, "3-D printing and rapid prototyping have created affordable ways to produce samples of human anatomy models and lab equipment, for example. 3-D models bring students and faculty together for dynamic learning opportunities."

FIGURE 12.2

Unity in action. Pepper is the world's first social programmable humanoid robot and is an outstanding example of how libraries are bringing people together around the big ideas of technology, creativity, and innovation.

Photograph: Courtesy of Carroll County (MD) Public Library

"We are beginning to see robots introduced in a variety of public spaces, such as our local grocery stores. Our goal is to support a broader understanding of positive interactions with robots, their strengths and current limitations, and how the underlying technologies work," says Jen Bishop, emerging and digital technologies manager at Carroll County (MD) Public Library.

"Real unity is desired by the human heart. It strives to labour creatively and actively, for its labour is a source of joy . . . it wants to rejoice what is common to all, what uplifts all, and what leads to a radiant future," said Nicholas Roerich, a Russian painter and writer.

"It seems to me that there is in each of us a capacity to comprehend the impressions and emotions which have been experienced by [hu]mankind from the beginning. Each individual has a subconscious memory of the green earth and murmuring waters, blindness and deafness cannot rob him [or her] of this gift from past generations. This inherited capacity is a sort of sixth sense . . . which sees, hears, feels, all in one,"[5] writes Helen Keller in her autobiography.

Does the library own a copy of Keller's *The Story of My Life* to guide people to her insights into the big ideas? Whether a library has online access to Emerson's essays or a print version sitting on the shelf, students can connect with the big idea of unity. It doesn't matter if people find a copy of *The Autobiography of Benjamin Franklin* as an inexpensive paperback edition in the biographies section or discover *The Papers of Benjamin Franklin* compiled and published in forty-two costly volumes in the humanities section: people can build a bridge to the big idea of humility and many other ideas. The key is for the librarian to connect people to these resources. The exploration and penetration of big ideas is up to the individual to do the work, but the librarian can act as the catalyst.

We can only be nurtured by the intangibles of life; that is, the big ideas. Libraries offer abundant treasures of intangible gifts that we need to read to nurture our own growth. We are meant to let big ideas lift us up in order to be the best librarians we can be.

NOTES

1. Alexander Pope, *An Essay on Criticism*, Poetry Foundation, https://www.poetry foundation.org/articles/69379/an-essay-on-criticism.
2. Ralph Waldo Emerson, *Essays and Poems by Ralph Waldo Emerson* (New York: Barnes and Noble Classics, 2004), 12–13.
3. Richard Louv, *Last Child in the Woods: Saving Our Children from Nature-Deficit Disorder* (Chapel Hill, NC: Algonquin Books of Chapel Hill, 2008), 98.
4. Benjamin Franklin, *The Autobiography & Other Writings* (New York: Bantam Classics, 1982), 85.
5. Helen Keller, *The Story of My Life* (1903; New York: Bantam Classics, 2005), 87–88.

Afterword

The best evidence that big ideas are permeating humanity lies in the works of excellence in the arts, literature, science, technology, business, education, and government. The library is an outstanding source of big ideas. Do we recognize that the library is a treasure of big ideas? Do we see its potential to help people rise from individual to whole, as Alexander Pope advocates? "If you look at them from the point of view of their differences, then there is . . . Ch'u and Yueh. But if you look at them from the point of their sameness, then the ten thousand things are all one," wrote Chuang Tzu, a Chinese philosopher in the fourth century AD.

Common sense should strongly suggest that when the library celebrates big ideas, this can lead to a renaissance of thinking. Celebrating big ideas can spark a renaissance in a person in which their mind becomes aware of its own potential. When we celebrate big ideas, we can create a renewal of our own understanding as we look for deeper levels of purpose. Just like in the European Renaissance, big ideas today lead to the essence of thought.

All of us have the option to be kinder and more respectful and to express goodwill—a small sample of big ideas that we can learn about through reading Plato, Pope, Shakespeare, Emerson, Dickinson, Browning, Keller, and many other great thinkers. A librarian is meant to be proactive about connecting the big ideas of optimism, humor, reverence, and more to the people we serve.

A higher level of ideas or abstract thought can lead library staff to gain insight into serving their communities. In this way, a library can help reinvigorate a declining community, college, or school by sparking curiosity in its residents and students to discover the joy of learning. A library can strengthen a sagging economy by jump-starting individual talent, offering self-directed education and technology resources, and promoting the entrepreneurial spirit. Libraries can help cultivate the value of courage and intelligent risk-taking, promote maturity and hard work, and help create and sustain healthy communities.

The Proto-Indo-European root *weid*—from which the word *idea* derives—means "to see." From the Greek, the word *idea* indicates a vision or reflection. These word origins suggest that an idea lies in the inner essence of understanding. It is, as Plato conveyed, a pattern of brilliance and wisdom. This level of abstract thinking offers the ability to see, understand, and apply the intangibles of life, such as patience, unity, and integrity, to everyday activity.

Big ideas have the ability to grow and develop. Although this is the end of the book, it challenges us to a new beginning of the growth of big ideas. It's not just that we read this book, and therefore, we're now done. It requires a transformation of attitudes, assumptions, and principles. Libraries of all types should be instrumental in this bigger-picture thinking.

How does the monarch butterfly know where to travel, how to navigate, and what to do when it arrives in an overwintering location, such as Mexico? The instinct of a butterfly to fly 1,000 or 2,000 miles to a warmer environment demonstrates a miraculous ability to respond to the patterns and rhythms of its nature. In just the same way, people seek and interact with ideas and concepts to fulfill their nature and produce wondrous results, such as creating libraries to enlighten humanity.

Few in today's world are better suited than a librarian to share ideas to help people improve their skills at living. Library staff are poised to help solve the seeming mysteries of abstract thinking in order to guide people to tap and use ideas to enrich life.

When a school librarian hands a seventh-grade student a copy of Franklin's autobiography, he or she can scatter joy. It can truly be a life-changing experience. When a high school student struggles to read Shakespeare for the first time—hey nonny nonny! It's an introduction to a treasure trove of big ideas. When a college student studies Plato's *The Republic* as required reading but then discovers and explores the other dialogues of Plato in the campus library—eureka! It's a transformative opportunity. When a public librarian promotes Keller's books as a reminder that life offers unlimited possibilities no matter what the obstacles—hope springs eternal! It's an invitation for young and old to explore the power of optimism and to reorganize our thinking, values, and outlook.

Through libraries, we can connect people to the intangibles of life, making these ideas accessible for anyone to explore and learn to express in their daily activities. If we let big ideas ferment our thinking, they will inaugurate a lifetime pursuit and a dignified and virtuous interplay with big ideas. All human beings are designed to open their hearts to the best within themselves and others—and seek to make civilization as great as possible. Higher-level or abstract thinking is a means to make that happen and is a cause for joyous celebration. We celebrate Plato's "the good," Socrates's "the examined life," Franklin's "doorways to wisdom," and Carnegie's admonition "let there be light." During life's challenges and opportunities, big ideas add a kind of grace and strength that can help us to endure and triumph.

Every library can help its users to know where to look and harvest big ideas. Many great writers have presented big ideas so clearly and compellingly that all we have to do is read and think about them. Each person has the work of stocking their own bookshelf of big ideas, but in this way, a big idea becomes ours—a cause for celebration.

APPENDIX

Suggested Reading

Aristotle. *Nicomachean Ethics*, trans. and ed. Joe Sachs. Newburyport, MA: Focus Publishing, R. Pullins, 2002.

Cole, John Y. *America's Greatest Library*. Washington, DC: Library of Congress, 2017.

De Bono, Edward. *The Mechanism of Mind*. London: Vermilion, 2015.

Emerson, Ralph Waldo. *Essays*. Reading, PA: Spencer, 1936. Or any copy of Emerson's *Essays*.

Franklin, Benjamin. *The Autobiography of Benjamin Franklin & Other Writings*. New York: Bantam Books, 1982. Or any copy of Franklin's autobiography.

Keller, Helen. *Optimism*. Atlanta, GA: Enthea. First published in 1903. This edition issued in 2006.

Keller, Helen. *The Story of My Life*. New York: Bantam Classics. First published in 1903. This edition issued in 2005.

Plato. *Plato: Complete Works*, ed. John M. Cooper. Indianapolis, IN: Hackett, 1997. Or any copy of Plato's works.

About the Authors

DOROTHY STOLTZ is the director for community engagement at the Carroll County (MD) Public Library and works to connect people of all ages with resources to enhance their lifelong learning. She is the coauthor of several books for the American Library Association, such as *Transform and Thrive: Ideas to Invigorate Your Library and Community* (2018). She has written numerous articles, including "Augmented Reality Brings Early Industry to Life" in the *Old Mill News*, and co-authored a white paper, "Media Mentorship in Libraries Serving Youth." She is an active member of the Library Leadership & Management Association, the Public Library Association, and the Association for Library Service to Children.

Coauthors

MORGAN MILLER is the director of the Cecil County (MD) Public Library, an award-winning educational institution that received the 2015 IMLS National Medal for Libraries. She is a member of the editorial board for *Public Libraries* magazine. Miller is active in library leadership throughout Maryland and recently coauthored a chapter in the book *Re-Envisioning the MLS* (2018), titled "Creating a New Era of Opportunity for All: How Librarians Can Lead Us There."

LISA PICKER is the director of communications for the Carroll County (MD) Public Library. She holds degrees in art with a concentration in art history and contemporary communications, and has fifteen years' experience in communications. She successfully attracts fifteen to twenty national bestselling authors to visit Carroll County each year, to the delight of library users. Picker's successful marketing strategies have made the Carroll County Public Library one of the highest circulating libraries per capita in the state of Maryland for the past fifteen years.

JOSEPH THOMPSON is the director of public services for the Carroll County (MD) Public Library. He formerly served as the senior administrator for public services at the Harford County (MD) Public Library, associate director of the Western Maryland Regional Library, and project coordinator for Maryland AskUsNow! Thompson served as the 2014–2015 president of the Reference and User Services Association and was president of the Maryland Library Association in 2018–2019. He received his MLS degree from the University of Maryland College Park in 2001.

CARRIE WILLSON is the executive director of the Calvert Library in Calvert County, Maryland. She has an enthusiasm for community-building and a commitment to removing barriers and delivering exceptional customer service at the library's four locations. Willson has served in a variety of leadership roles with the Maryland Library Association and currently serves on the board of directors for the Public Library Association (PLA) and the PLA's Legislation and Advocacy Committee.

Index